KETO DIET FOR

BEGINNERS:

TOP 61 FANTASTIC AND SIMPLE RECIPES IN ONE KETOGENIC COOKBOOK,

EASY RECIPES FOR YOUR MEAL TIME

Donovan Ekstrom

© 2018

TABLE OF CONTENTS

INTRODUCTION

Do you suffer from diabetes? Obesity? I am here to tell you just what the "Experts" Fitness Gurus, and Bro Science people are not telling you, and most importantly don't want you to know: All the lies and misinformation is crap, you don't need any of what they are selling to maximize your potential and build muscle that lasts.

- You don't need to shell out hard earned cash on dangerous supplements that aren't regulated by the FDA or even take steroids.
- You don't need to go on the latest fad diet, follow points or eat 100 calories a day to lose weight.
- You don't need to practice "muscle confusion" to keep making gains in and out of the gym.
- Learn why "Clean" eating is a myth and what you can do about it.
- You don't need boring hours of cardio, or dangerous 300 bpm heart rate routines that can leave you tired, stale or worse.
- You don't need to worry about "cheat" foods or eating less.

- You don't need to spend endless hours in the gym with no gains.

Those are just a small snippet of the myths and tales that keep women and men from maximizing their potential in weight loss, building muscle mass, or keeping fit.

In this book you're going to learn something most men and women will never know...

The exact step by step plan of muscle and eating right that makes losing 10 to 20 pounds of fat while building lean, sexy muscle a breeze...and it only takes 2 -3 weeks.

This book reveals things like...

The biggest fat loss myths & mistakes that keep men and women overweight, frustrated, and ultimately give up.

Easy to make recipes that will keep you on track so you can build muscle, get lean and toned, lose fat, fix "problem" areas and more.

The lies men and women are told about how to "tone" and "shape" their bodies, and what you REALLY need to do to have sexy, lean curves.

How to master the "Mindset" of keeping fit and have self-discipline and confidence and the willpower to succeed.

How to eat the foods you love and still lose weight and keep it off.

And a whole lot more!

Here is what I recommend to you before we get started: forget all you ever heard about fitness and dieting. That may sound a little blunt and it is, but believe me you'll thank me later.

Keto Diet for Beginners is about freedom from the misinformation that is out there and flies in the face of bad dieting advice as well. Throughout the book you may read some things you thought were okay to do, and some things you still think are not okay to do, just follow along and trust me, actions speak louder than words, talk is cheap. But I know you won't need to follow another "expert" or false trainer again.

You ready? Let's get started!

CHAPTER 1: WHAT IS THE KETOGENIC DIET?

A ketogenic diet, also known as "Keto," is where you cut back on your intake of carbohydrates in order for your body to burn fat. This is very different from diets where you starve yourself crash dieting, or you go so long without carbohydrates that you are left on low carb island forever.

Keto involves minimizing your consumption of carbohydrates by getting rid of the foods that are making you fat. Doing this will put your body into a state of what is called Ketosis. This is actually where the ketogenic diet gets its name from. Next I will explain just what "Ketosis" is; there is a lot of misinformation when it comes to ketosis.

Ketosis – Explained

Isn't ketosis dangerous? Contrary to what you heard ketosis is a very natural state for the body to be in. Most people experience a condition called ketosis when they suddenly go from a high-carbohydrate diet to a low-carbohydrate diet. This occurs when ketone molecules are circulating in the blood in a higher amount than on the previous high-carbohydrate diet. This is contrary to the myths, distortions, and lies pushed by vegetarians and other high-carbohydrate diet supporters. Ketosis allows the body to function efficiently and live off of stored body fat when necessary. Ketones are not a poison which is how most medical and nutritional experts refer to them. Ketones make the body run more efficiently and are a fuel source for the brain.

What the "experts" refer to as Ketoacidosis is a life-threatening condition commonly associated with Type 1 diabetes and insulin-dependent Type 2 diabetes. Ketoacidosis is not the same as normal dietary ketosis. The abnormally low level of insulin in the diabetic can sometimes lead to a toxic build-up of blood glucose, causing excess urination, thirst, and dehydration. The glucose cannot enter the cells to produce energy in the absence of insulin. This causes the body to break down an excessive amount of body fat and muscle tissues for energy. Then Ketoacidosis becomes an unhealthy condition in which the body has excessively high glucose and ketone bodies at the same time. This condition could never happen to a normal non-diabetic on a reduced carbohydrate diet.

Normal ketosis and lipolysis stabilizes blood glucose within a normal range and prevents the breakdown of healthy muscle tissue. The dietary restriction of carbohydrates prevents any build-up of excess glucose. The blood glucose level remains perfectly normal and stable. The body is actually powered normally by ketone bodies while we sleep. As you see a high fat diet and ketosis are fuel for the body and not damaging such as when you are in the unhealthy state of burning glucose (sugar) for energy which leads to hyperinsulism (abnormal insulin levels) and, diabetes, heart disease, and strokes

The Keto diet will allow you to be in a lipolysis state and reach ketosis in the body, and this is the sweet spot for losing all that unsightly body fat and weight that you have been trying so hard to lose. Remember I said I would make it easy for you to understand, so lipolysis comes first then ketosis, your burning fat for energy. Ketosis happens because you are taking in a reduced amount of carbohydrates and you don't need to go that low for this to happen. This process begins on the first day of your weight loss plan on the Keto Diet.

Just remember that lipolysis is a state you are in when burning fat as energy when you reduce carbohydrates and that ketosis is natural, and you are not going to get sick as some may have led you to believe.

There have been many styles of reduced carbohydrate diets and some work and some don't. Some of them take you so low in carbohydrates that you are just left out in the cold and feel lost, you never have this feeling because there is total dietary freedom.

With the Keto Diet you start at 100 grams of carbs per day. However, if you want to speed up the process you start out at 50 grams a day. Everybody is different, but the one factor remains the same rapid weight loss awaits you. You never have to worry about counting calories or taking shakes or pills. I'll break down carbohydrates for you and how to keep track. Just take it easy and let everything fall into place.

Just Do It

"I still don't get lipolysis." Its okay, I know I have said a mouthful, and it just means that you're burning up the fat you have been eating instead of carbohydrate (sugar) foods such as bread and oatmeal, rice and the like.

When your body is in ketosis you may smell a fruity odor on your breathe which is normal. When people eat less carbohydrate, their bodies turn to fat for energy, so it makes sense that more ketones are generated. Some of those ketones (acetoacetate and B-hydroxybutyrate) are used for energy; the heart muscle and kidneys, for example, prefer ketones to glucose. Most cells, including the brain cells, are able to use ketones for their energy. But there is one type of ketone molecule, called acetone that cannot be used and is excreted as waste, mostly in the urine and breath which is responsible for the funny breathe you may smell. This is an indicator that you are losing weight and burning up stored body fat for energy. When you reduce you r carbohydrates you are in lipolysis.

Lipolysis is just what you have been looking for in losing weight and beats low fat high carb any day, and best of all you distance yourself from diseases associated with eating the old way such as, heart disease and diabetes. Fatigue and depression all become a thing of the past once you cross over into a lypolytic state. And make no mistake this has been well documented it is not quackery, doctors and researchers have known this about the body for decades, but the truth got distorted along the way for profit and other reasons.

Fat or Sugar for Fuel

There is a misconception that you need carbohydrates to have energy. The truth is, fat is the preferred fuel for humans and has been for most of human history. The liver can actually produce small amounts of glucose to keep our bodies stable on a daily basis. Here is where ketones come in. They are taken from the fat you eat and that is when you become a lipolytic fat burner, when this state of lipolysis is happening your vital organs that run on fat such as the brain, heart and so on are in a preferred state. So theses so called "evil" ketones we have falsely been led to believe are fueling the body, much in the same way a high carbohydrate eater is fueled by over eating high sugary foods. Glucose (sugar) and ketones are sources of energy to the body but one is better and that is fat.

What is better to think about is whether you want to be a fat burner or a sugar burner, burning fat is the most fastest and best way to look and feel your best, and best of all you lose weight without setting foot in a gym or slaving away on faulty diet plans.

Importantly there are those even your own doctor who unknowingly will try to convince you that you must eat carbohydrates daily for fuel and there is fast and slow burning carbohydrates, that may be true that some carbohydrates would burn slower in the body, but you are still eating sugar in the end because carbohydrates break down into the body at some point as sugar and your body has to deal with that, and you unnecessarily create high insulin levels And this is where disease begins, why a diabetic would be recommended to eat a high carbohydrate diet when sugar is what got him there in the first place is a crime.

Our bodies have been efficiently been able to run off fat for much of our history, it was only until that last 10,000 years when agriculture began that we started eating carbohydrates, and never in history as in the 20th century where we began to eat sugar like it was going out of style.

Once you begin to reduce your carbohydrates and eat more fat and go back to your roots the weight falls off easily and effortlessly and you will see that there could have never been a better way. Insulin within the body converts all the high sugar you eat into body fat and this is not normal which is why you see all that fat accumulating and cellulite becomes the norm. When you eat a high fat reduced carbohydrate diet, fat and ketones are used up and readily available as an energy source to the body. However, when you are always eating a low fat high carb diet you never reach a healthy level of ketosis within the body and thus never lose weight and keep it off. You look and feel awful. Once you eat more fat and reduce your carbohydrates you won't release insulin with the chronic yo-yoing and detrimental effects of storing body fat you are out of this bad cycle.

Once you begin to eat this way and fat makes up your preferred energy source a lot of things will begin to happen, you must understand this, you are reversing the aging process, you will begin to feel young again, the desire for sex, feeling confident and direct, clothes fit again, and unlike the low fat high carb diet you retain muscle tone and elasticity to your skin giving you a permanent youthful appearance. You did hear that right, fat gives elasticity to your skin giving you a youthful appearance. Here are some of the many benefits to eating a diet high in fat:

Fats will provide all the energy you need. Think about it carbohydrates have 4 calories per gram as well as protein, but fat carries 9 calories per gram making it a more efficient powerhouse of energy to the body.

Fat is vital to every organ in the body. Your major organs such as the brain, heart, kidneys and many others run on fat and cushion organs from damage. Without fat you are doing your body an injustice and the effects of this low fat eating can be seen already, ever wonder why you can't think or feel you may have early Alzheimer's?

Fats help the body absorb vitamins. Many vitamins are fat soluble such as A, D, E, and K. This means that fat is needed for these vitamins to be absorbed and not a one a day fish oil capsule is not going to cut it.

Fats make sex hormones normal. Once you eat a diet high in fat you will start to notice that you feel horny again or sexy, and this is normal because fat regulates production of testosterone and estrogen within the body, and most know that once you reach a certain age menopause and andropause (male) become the norm, but only if you are eating the low fat high carb way. In fact age related menopause and male andropause are stopped dead in their track, and best of all you boost low hormones naturally without synthetic chemical drugs such as testosterone and estrogen which have been known to cause breast and uterus cancer and balding and prostate cancer in men.

Fat gives elasticity to skin. When you eat a low fat diet one of the first things you notice is that your skin is more dry, and flaky, and you have more wrinkles. You even have lost muscle tone despite lifting weights and well you look like hell. Fat will make your skin retain its youthful appearance and keep muscle tone and best of all give you that youthful vitality, even when losing all that extra weight, it doesn't matter if you lose 100 or 200 pounds you still keep that great looking skin and you're doing it from the inside out. Remember skin is made up of fat, so when you reduce dietary fat you know the answer and conclusion.

Ketosis is a safe and normal process in the human body. When you eat very little carbohydrate, the body will not use glucose anymore and burn up all its reserves, then your body will start to burn excess fat on the body, rather than relying on glucose for energy you burn up fats, and you build up ketones in the body.

Keto Flu

Some people experience discomfort after the first few days of doing keto, this is not typical and not everyone gets this thing known as the "keto flu." However, you should know what to watch out for and how to combat these feelings if you do get them. The reason why some call it the "flu" is because the symptoms can feel somewhat like the flu initially. It's temporary and usually rears its ugly head at about days 3 thru 5, and is over fairly quickly, there is a quick fix that can make you feel better in 10 minutes, and that is more water and salt.

Here are some symptoms to watch out for:

- Heart palpitations
- Tired
- Headache
- Dizzy or lightheadedness (especially when standing)
- Nausea and vomiting
- Muscle cramps
- Dry mouth
- Anxiety
- Anger

Causes of the Keto Flu

The keto flu is caused by the body making the changes over to burning up stored body fat for energy instead of using sugar as energy for the body.

Most of these symptoms are caused by the body getting dehydrated, you tend to lose a lot of water and salt and electrolytes on keto at the start, because you pee more and as the body gets into ketosis (fat burning mode).

Again, this can be fixed with a few simple tips.

Top Tips forgetting Rid of The Keto Flu

Drink more water

During the first week of keto, if you drink more water and add some salt to your water you can eliminate the keto flu symptoms quite easily. Take a ½ of a teaspoon of salt and mix it into some water and this will make you feel better in about 10 minutes. You can do this two times a day.

Another alternative is to drink bouillon, Knorr makes a great powder chicken broth found in most supermarkets. You can mix a small spoon in a glass with warm or hot water and add some salted butter and sip it slowly. This will make you feel better fast and it tastes great as well.

Adding more fat into your diet

Adding salt usually helps with keto flu symptoms, but if you still feel not well, you may be not eating enough fat.

We tend to slowly go back to our old ways on keto, not really realizing that we are eating a low fat, low carb diet, and this is an easy way to get keto flu. Your body will go into starvation mode and you will get tired, hungry, and feel awful.

If you are doing the keto diet right, you are getting enough fats with meals, you're not hungry as much after meals, and you have a lot of energy. Up your fat at the start of keto and once you have been doing it for a while you can cut back on the fat a little.

In short: add more fat when you can to your diet and salt, and drink water.

Adding a little bit of carbs

You have been adding more salt and drinking water till you can float, and you still feel terrible? If you honestly tried the other tips then you can easily ease the symptoms by adding some carbohydrates into your diet.

Make the transition more slowly over to keto, eat a little bit more carbs, say you've been eating 15 grams of carbs all week and you feel like hell, try taking in 50 grams a day and see how you feel, this is perfectly fine and within low carb limits, for example many take in much more than this in one day even in one sitting, in the carb ranges of 300 to 1000 grams!

You can eat a banana as long as you don't go over your daily carb count. The "experts" say our bodies are made up of 70% water so with that try to get in a little more water than usual in the first couple of weeks. If you are an avid exerciser you may need more, and I suggest at these times that you ingest a rehydration drink with glucose and electrolytes so you don't get dizzy when doing your triathlons and such, but only at these times because some of these drinks have too much sugar (remember your daily carb count). However you can find great alternative zero calorie and carb free electrolyte drinks just check your local supermarket or go online. PowerAde makes a great tasting zero carb drink for rehydration while working out. Eating a little bit more carbs may slow down your weight loss but not by much and the keto flu won't be a problem.

CHAPTER 2 KETO KEY POINTS

AVOIDING PITFALLS

If you have decided to try the keto diet out, you should be well acquainted with certain key points. Here are the two caveats keep in mind:

Be Strong the First Week, reducing your carbs will be tough, but if you follow this to a T you will lose weight, trust me. You will be in fat burning mode in as little as one day as your body will burn up any remaining glucose that is left in your body and will zap fat stores. If you cheat or do a low fat diet one day then keto the next, you will switch your metabolism back to burning sugar and storing fat, and make it that much harder on yourself, so don't do it.

Consume more vitamin rich vegetables and stay properly hydrated, eating more vegetables will provide your body with nutrients , electrolytes and vitamins that the body needs while on keto, plus if you are drinking enough water that pesky keto flu won't even be a problem.

SPECIAL TIPS

The first few weeks of keto can be quite hard; your cravings will be strong for something sweet. Sugar may be a problem for some. If you find yourself craving carbohydrates during the first two weeks treat yourself to as much diet soda as you like, and use whip cream and sugar free Jell-O and desserts, these are great ways to fight cravings. Even the recipes later on in the dessert section are great for this. Have the willpower to see yourself through and you will succeed. There are many books which are devoted to low carb and keto way of eating, but I'd like to recommend you the "The Atkins Diet" 1972 version by Dr. Robert Atkins M.D. This is a really great book, and best of all it really is strict in the carbohydrate levels of the keto diet. The other versions are great as well but 1972 is the best if you are serious about keto.

This book will help you to stay on track, type this link below to checkout the contents of this book.

http://bit.ly/atkinsd

MOTIVATION
The Five Cornerstones of the Keto Diet

Weight will be lost – The weight will melt off your body in record time. Fat loss is indiscriminate when you eat the right way, for both men and women. Do not feel at a loss for any reason if you fall off and eat the old way, just get right back on the diet after that last meal.

Staying In Shape Year Round – This means that you will maintain your weight instead of getting in shape for summer, or just the weekend, with the Keto Diet you look good all the time and it shows! Even friends and family will compliment you on your new look. Most other diets only allow you to get in shape for a short period of time with calorie counts and meal plans, but they don't last, plus you end up bloated from all the high starchy foods you would have to eat to maintain the lost weight. This is not a diet where you lose and gain like a yo-yo and the process, these starvation diets become so rigid and burdensome that you give up in sheer frustration.

Your health will improve – The feelings you get on the Keto Diet is not only physical but psychological as well. Just by not eating all the sugary foods in high quantity and replacing them with healthy fat delicious meals you become full of energy and life. Once your body has made the shift to fat burning mode and no longer runs on the old carbohydrate damaging metabolism, with chronic high blood sugar levels and mood swings, you will feel it. Once I gave up the standard American way of eating with the recommended food guide pyramid everything changed and for the better, and it was fast too! I began looking and feeling good right from the start. And best of all you will prevent disease within your body; and you will feel good doing it.

Appetite Control – Ever been on a diet where you just wanted to eat everything in site? Well not with the Keto Diet. The fact of the matter is that with this new way of eating you simply cut carbs, and your appetite tends to go down and this results in you eating much fewer calories without trying.

Reversing Metabolic Syndrome – Low Carb diets such as Keto are the most effective ways of eating to reverse and prevent Metabolic Syndrome.

Metabolic Syndrome is a medical condition that leads to all sorts of chaos and pain throughout the body, many disorders happen from this disease such as diabetes and heart disease.

Symptoms of Metabolic Syndrome:

- Abdominal obesity
- High blood pressure >125
- High fasting blood sugar levels >99
- High triglyceride Levels in the blood
- Very low HDL levels

The best part of the ketogenic diet besides permanent weight loss is all five of these problems are quickly fixed on this diet.

NUTRIENTS TO INCLUDE IN THE KETO DIET

Before we get into the juicy details of the recipes, we need to cover the most commonly used ingredients and stuff to avoid. Knowing this will get you started on the right track

What to Eat

The Keto diet is focused on providing your body with the best natural whole foods it needs, and getting rid of the food that has been causing your body to gain excessive weight and bring on the unsightly body fat that won't go away. If you want fast weight loss remember that in in the beginning you need to keep your carbohydrates to 30 grams a day and no more. Remember that you can stir fry, sauté, deep fry, or grill and a little flour or breading is okay as long as you don't go over your carb count for the day. During the week, eat plenty of fat and meat with vegetables and less carbs and you should be okay. Here is a list of foods you can eat.

For most meals you can eat any of the following as much as you want:

Meat:

Beef (steak with fat on, and hamburger full fat), pork, ham (spam), hot dogs, bacon, goat, lamb, sausage, pepperoni, salami, prosciutto.

Poultry: Duck, chicken (fat/skin on), quail, and turkey (not lean).

Fish: Any type okay, including salmon, tuna, trout, flounder.

Shellfish: Clams, oysters, snail, scallops, crab, lobster, abalone.

Whole eggs: Don't separate the yolks, cook any style, poached, hardboiled, fried in lard or butter.

Cheeses and Yogurt

You can eat almost any type of cheese, along with yogurt just be sure to remember that some spreads and cheeses such as cottage cheese contain carbs, as well as most yogurts, just be sure to get full fat.

Provolone, cheddar, Gouda, cream cheese, sour cream, goat, Swiss, blue cheeses are all great.

Yogurt, any kinds just get full fat and count the carbs.

Vegetables and Salads

Eat as much as you want but refer to the vegetable carbohydrate counter at the back of the book to see which ones have the most.

Salad Toppings

Don't worry about what you put on top of your salad most dressings are low in carb count anyway so check labels, if your out meeting with friends for lunch disregard carb counting just enjoy yourself. There are a variety of toppings to choose from such as bacon, cheese, eggs, mushrooms, seeds, nuts, oils (olive and vegetable) raisins (don't go overboard).

Soups and Bouillon

Soup is okay, just watch the minestrone or vegetable and potato varieties especially ones coming out of a can. Clam chowder can be okay as long as you take into consideration the carbohydrate count. Bouillon and clear broths are especially good on this diet because the sodium (salt) intake helps with fatigue and electrolytes.

Spices and Herbs

Feel free to add spices and herbs to lively up your food as much as you want, they literally have no carbohydrates. Check labels of your favorite hot sauce because some have carbs, but not too much to make and impact on your weight loss. Remember make it fun.

Cooking oil and Fats

I am a big fan of lard and olive oil (extra virgin) as they cook well and make food taste fantastic. Lard is actually good for the body; some of you are probably going "eww" well check out the profile from the nutrition label on the lard. There are 12 grams of fat per serving, but only 5 grams of saturated fat. About half the fat in lard is monosaturated -you know the kind of fat that supposedly makes olive oil good for us. The saturated fat, of course, will primarily raise your HDL levels and that is a good thing if you ask me. The fatty-acid profile of lard is very similar to human body fat. And if you lose weight and consume your own fat in the process, that's good for you.

Butter is great, added salt or unsalted is fine. Stay away from fake butters such margarine and vegetable oil butters, except if it is olive oil butter, however it must be 100% olive oil not 40 percent and the rest vegetable oil. I tell you to stay away from make believe butter not because they contain carbs but because of that pesky trans-fat (hydrogenated oils) that have been getting talked about lately. They are seriously not good for you and should not be included in anyone's diet.

When it comes to the fat on the meat please do not remove the valuable fat off like a surgeon, not only will the food taste bland but your missing out on precious fats ability to help you burn up stored body fat. So keep the steak fat on, the chicken skin, and bacon strips fat also. Remember were not following the low fat dogma high carbohydrate diet anymore.

How Do You Like The Book So Far?

http://bit.ly/ketode

If you're undecided, just leave a review later...

Chapter 3: Recipes. Smoothies and Breakfast Meals

Here, are 61 fantastic recipes that will help you to enjoy your food while dieting. There will be recipes for breakfast, smoothies, lunch, dinner and snacks so you can have tasty delicious treats whenever you wish.

Let's start with some of the most delicious smoothie and breakfast recipes that will get you off to a great start of a day.

1. Breakfast Yoghurt

Serves 2 - Prep time: 5 minutes Cook time: 8 minutes

Ingredients:

- 2 cup of full fat Greek yoghurt
- 4 drops of liquid stevia (vanilla is delicious!)
- A few almonds or a pinch of shredded coconut for each bowl

Instructions:

1. Scoop the yoghurt into a bowl.

2. Add a few drops of stevia and stir. (Go easy on the stevia, a little really goes a long way)

3. Top with a few almonds.

4. A pinch of shredded coconut is also a tasty way to liven up this quick and easy breakfast.

Nutrition Per Serving

Calories: 145 Fat: 13 g Net Carbohydrates: 2 g Protein: 2 g

2. AVOCADO GREEN SMOOTHIE

Serves 2 / Prep time: 10 minutes

I just love smoothies and many think that when you eat low carb, Carb Cycle or a Ketogenic Diet you just can't have smoothies anymore. This is not true. Depending on how much weight you want to lose, a smoothie here and there is not going to hurt, and the apples I have added to this mix is beneficial as it provides vitamins and minerals are body needs.

Ingredients:

- 2 cups of carrageenan free, unsweetened almond milk
- 1 avocado

- 2 green apples peeled and diced to make blending easier
- A handful of spinach
- 2 drops of liquid stevia each serving

Instructions:

1. Add the avocado, green apple and spinach to your blender.
2. Pour in the almond milk. If desired, you can add ice cubes to the mix.
3. Add a couple drops of stevia.
4. For a protein boost, add a scoop of organic nut butter, your choice.
5. To increase your veggie intake, add slices of cucumber or other green. Enjoy!

Nutrition Per Serving 375 Calories 25g of Fat 30g of Protein 4g of Net Carbs

3. VANILLA GOODNESS SMOOTHIE

Serves 1 - Prep time: 5 minutes

Here is a super fast and easy recipe that I like in the morning when I am on the go. You can add stevia, or whatever sweetener you like. Remember whatever I list as ingredients feel free to omit or add your own twists. Enjoy!

Ingredients:

- 2 cups full fat Greek yoghurt (preferably organic)
- ½ cup almond milk
- Vanilla powder or real vanilla scraped from a vanilla pod (recommended)
- A few drops of Stevia
- Ice Cubes

Instructions:

1. Pour all of the ingredients into a blender.
2. Blend until smooth. Enjoy a glass in the sun, or on the way to work for a fast and nourishing breakfast.

4. PEANUT BUTTER CUP SMOOTHIE

Serves 4 - Prep time: 10 minutes Cook time: 10 minutes

Lovers of the popular candy featuring chocolate and peanut butter will enjoy the same flavor combination for breakfast or a filling snack. For a more chocolaty taste, add a teaspoon of good-quality cocoa powder and a couple drops of liquid stevia. These additions will not add any fat, protein, or carbs to the smoothie, just 3 calories per serving.

In

t milk

ate protein powder

- 2 tablespoons peanut butter (sugar free is preferable but with a sugar is okay)
- 3 ice cubes

Instructions:

1. Put the water, coconut cream, protein powder, peanut butter, and ice in a blender and blend until smooth.
2. Pour into 2 glasses and serve immediately.

Nutrition Per Serving Calories: 520; Fat: 50; Protein: 47; Carbs: 8g; Fiber: 10g; Net Carbs: 2g

5. KETO BREAKFAST ROLLS

These rolls are great for breakfast and are super easy to make. You can simply double the recipe and save em in the freezer for later. I like to eat these for breakfast with real butter, or you can cut tomatoes and mozzarella and drizzle salt and cracked pepper onto them, delicious.

Ingredients:

- 1.5 cups almond flour
- 2/3 cup of powdered psyllium husk
- ½ cup coconut flour
- ½ cup flaxseed meal
- 2 teaspoons of cream of tartar
- 2 teaspoons of garlic and/or onion powder
- 1 teaspoon of baking powder
- 1 teaspoon of sea salt
- Seeds for topping the finished rolls
- 6-7 egg whites
- 2 whole eggs
- 2 cups of warm water

Instructions:

1. Preheat oven to 350 degrees Fahrenheit.
2. Mix all dry ingredients except powdered psyllium and seeds in a bowl.
3. Mix the psyllium powder in a separate bowl with the egg whites, the 2 whole eggs and the 2 cups of warm water.

4. Combine the two bowls into one and mix using a hand mixer.

5. When the ingredients are well combined, form rolls using your hands and a spoon.

6. Sprinkle the rolls with your choice of seeds (sesame, pumpkin, sunflower, etc.)

7. Place them on a baking sheet with parchment paper leaving enough space between the rolls to rise and expand.

8. Bake for 45 minutes. Remove the rolls and allow to cool.

9. Feel free to add whatever you like on top, make a sandwich, add cream cheese, or slap mayonnaise on top and eat like that, yummy.

Nutrition Per Serving I don't have the calorie or much of the nutrition for these babies, but they come out to less than a gram of carbs each serving, I count each one as 1 gram of carbs just to be safe.

6. CREAM CHEESE PANCAKES WITH SUGAR FREE SYRUP

Serves 6 - Prep time: 5 minutes - Cook time: 10 minutes

Who said that you can't have pancakes on this diet? Well, I am here to tell you that you are going to love these. And best of all there isn't any wheat flour in them so if you are having gluten issues these won't affect at all.

Ingredients:

- 2 eggs
- 2 ounces of cream cheese
- 2 tbsps. of sour cream
- A few drops of liquid stevia
- Vanilla powder or a pinch of cinnamon
- Butter for frying

Instructions:

1. Blend the 2 eggs and the cream cheese.
2. Add the stevia and the spices.
3. Blend until smooth.
4. Heat and melt the butter in the frying pan.
5. Once the pan is hot, pour a pancake-sized amount of batter into the frying pan.
6. Once the sides are firm enough to flip (this should take about two minutes), flip the pancake and let it cook for another minute or until a nice golden brown color.
7. Enjoy with a bit of sour cream and/or a couple of berries.

Nutrition Per Serving Size: 5 pancakes Calories: 400 Fat: 32 Carbohydrates: 4g net Protein: 25

7. BREAKFAST CASSEROLE WITH SOUR CREAM

Serves 8 - Prep time: 5 minutes - Cook time: 35 minutes

Casserole is a great meal in the morning, the one thing about this recipe is it takes a little longer to make than the other recipes in the morning, but that's okay. I save this one for a Saturday or when I have a little more time in the kitchen. Takes 50 minutes to make, and the recipe will get you 2 servings, but it sure is hearty.

Ingredients:

- 5 eggs
- 3 cooked bacon strips, coarsely chopped
- 1 cup fresh baby spinach
- 1/2 cup butternut squash, chopped
- 1/2 cup fresh mushrooms, sliced
- 1/2 cup yellow squash, chopped
- 1/4 cup red onion, chopped
- 1 pinch garlic powder
- Salt and pepper to taste

Instructions:

Pre-heat the oven to 350 degrees.

1. Combine all the ingredients in a medium sized bowl except for the seasoning. Mix well.
2. Next, add garlic powder with salt and pepper to taste.
3. Brush the bottom and sides of the baking dish with coconut oil.
4. Pour in the mixture.
5. Put inside the pre-heated oven. Let it cook at 350 degrees for 45 minutes.
6. When cooked, place on a cooling rack, and then serve.

Nutrition Per Serving 1 serving Calories: 500 Fat: 40 Carbohydrates: 2g net Protein: 44

8. SAUSAGE AND EGGS

Serves 1 - Prep time: 5 minutes

Ingredients:

- 3-4 Sausage links Pork
- 2-3 eggs
- 3/4 cup heavy cream
- 3/4 cup shredded Cheddar cheese
- 2 tbsp. Sour Cream

Instructions:

1. Heat up a large iron pan, use medium heat, then add your favorite cooking oil, add the sausages and be careful not to burn them, turn them evenly, turn the heat down slightly.

2. Drain off fat once they are cooked and cut the into small sizes you like.

3. Place the sausage aside and start to bear the eggs and heavy cream together, you can use the sausage fat and the same pan to cook the eggs, add the cheddar cheese and cook to your liking, add the sausage and continue to stir the eggs and sausage together, make sure to not cook the eggs too long or they will be tough and not as tasty. Top with sour cream, salsa, or your favorite toppings and serve with low carb bread.

Nutrition Per Serving Size: 5 pancakes Calories: 400 Fat: 32 Carbohydrates: 4g net Protein: 25

Chapter 4: Recipes. Keto Snacks

9. Cheddar Cheese Fat Bombs

Makes 10 bombs - Prep time: 5 minutes, ½ hour chill time in fridge

These decadent Fat bombs are really neat because they are gluten and nut allergy free and will help to curb those pesky sugar cravings.

Ingredients:

- 2 ounces cheddar cheese
- 3 ounces cream cheese
- 5 tbsp. butter
- 7 slices of bacon

Instructions:

1. Cook the bacon to your liking, then chop into small pieces.
2. Place a baking sheet and a piece of parchment paper aside on your counter
3. Take a small bowl and stir the cheddar cheese, cream cheese, butter and bacon.

4. Use a large spoon to frop the mix onto your baking sheet.

5. Then place the sheet in the freezer until they get semi hard. About 30 minutes or so.

6. Store the bombs in a sealed container in the fridge for 1 week

Nutrition Per Serving Size: 1 bomb Calories: 72 Fat: 10g Net Carbohydrates: 0g net Protein: 4g

10. SMOKED SALMON BOMBS

Makes 12 fat bombs - Prep time: 5 minutes, 30 minutes chill time

Smoked salmon can be found at most club stores like Costco, Sam's and others, and your favorite supermarket. Yes, it is a little pricy at times, but I opt for cheaper varieties as they are entirely the same, it is a matter of taste really.

Ingredients:

- ½ cup cream cheese
- ½ cup butter
- 2-3 ounces smoked salmon
- 2 tsp lemon juice
- Crack of black pepper or fresh dill

Instructions:

1. Place a baking sheet and a piece of parchment paper aside on your counter

2. Take a small bowl and stir the cream cheese, butter, salmon and lemon juice.

3. Use a spoon and scoop the mixture onto your baking sheet. Ideally, you want to make 12 little bomb mounds.

4. Place the little bombs on your baking sheet in the fridge for 30 minutes, if not set yet shoot for an hour.

5. Store the bombs in container of your choice in the fridge for about 5 days.

Nutrition Per Serving Size: 1 bomb Calories: 69 Fat: 20g Net Carbohydrates: 0g net Protein: 10g

11. PIZZA FAT BOMBS

If you miss pizza, then you are sure to love this recipe. These make 6 fat bombs.

Ingredients:

- 14 pepperoni slices
- 2 tbsp. sun dried tomato pesto
- 4 oz. cream cheese

- 2 tbsp. chopped, fresh basil
- 8 black olives, pitted or veggie of choice
- Salt and pepper, to taste

Instructions:

1. Dice olives and pepperoni into small pieces.
2. Mix everything together.
3. Form into 6 balls and garnish with basil, veggies and pepperoni.
4. Enjoy this savory treat.

Nutrition Per Serving Size: 1 pizza slice Calories: 510 Fat: 57g Net Carbohydrates: 4g net Protein: 15g

12. CUCUMBER BOATS

Serves 1 - Prep time: 5 minutes Cook time: 5 minutes

Ingredients:

- 2 thin slices of cucumber cut lengthwise
- 2 pieces of cold cut meat, your choice
- 2 pieces of cheddar Cheese

Instructions:

1. Assemble a slice of cucumber with a cold cut slice and a piece of cheddar.
2. Roll them together. Repeat the process with the other pieces and eat on the go.
3. Serves 1 person (Double up ingredients for more)

Nutrition Per Serving Size: 1 boat Calories: 80 Fat: 8g Net Carbohydrates: 3g net Protein: 12g

13. AVOCADO AND EGG

Serves 4 - Prep time: 5 minutes Cook time: 5 minutes

Which came first the avocado or the egg? It doesn't matter. You are going to love these.

These make 1 serving.

Ingredients:

- 4 eggs
- 2 avocados
- A bit of salt and pepper
- Some butter for frying the eggs

Instructions:

1. Fry the eggs over the stove with some butter.

2. Slice the avocado in half, remove the seed and replace with the fried egg.

3. Repeat with the other egg and avocado half.

4. Season with a bit of salt and pepper. Bon appétit!

Nutrition Per Serving Size: 1 Avocado Egg Munchies Calories: 520 Fat: 45g Net Carbohydrates: 3g net Protein: 30g

14. CRAB CAKES

Serves 4 - Prep time: 10 minutes Cook time: 25 minutes

The secret I have found to perfect crab cakes is that you have to press em good, but be gentle when handling them or they will break apart.

Ingredients:

- 1/2 pound crab meat
- 1 medium egg
- 1/8 cup breadcrumbs (made from almond flour)
- 1 tablespoon olive oil
- 1 tablespoon mayonnaise
- 1/2 tablespoon diced celery
- 1/2 tablespoon minced onion
- 1/4 tablespoon minced garlic

- 1/2 teaspoon Old Bay Seasoning
- 1/2 teaspoon Dijon mustard
- Salt and pepper

Instructions:

1. Combine all ingredients except breadcrumbs and crab meat in a large bowl.
2. Mix well then add crab meat. Mix again then gradually add the breadcrumbs.
3. Scoop the mixture into equal portions.
4. Shape each portion into a ball and flatten to form half inch-thick cakes.
5. Heat a skillet on medium and add olive oil.
6. When the pan is hot, cook the crab cakes until each side is golden brown.
7. Cook two cakes at a time. Serve immediately!

Nutrition Per Serving Size: 1 cake Calories: 70 Fat: 5g Net Carbohydrates: 2g net Protein: 7g

15. MEXICAN CEVICHE

Serves 8 - Prep time: 15 minutes Cook time: 25 minutes

When I traveled to Mexico last year, I just loved Ceviche, you can find this on the beach at any resort in Mexico, but why not just make it now. I asked the owner of a restaurant I dined at in Mexico for the recipe and she gave it to me, but I added my own little twist. This recipe is good for 1 serving. Enjoy!

Ingredients:

- 1/4 pound halibut fillet
- 1 lime
- 1 jalapeno pepper, finely chopped
- 1/2 small onion, finely chopped
- 1/4 green bell pepper, finely chopped
- 1/4 cup fresh tomato, finely sliced
- 1 tablespoon chopped parsley
- Chopped fresh cilantro, to taste
- 1/2 tablespoon white vinegar
- 1/8 teaspoon oregano
- Salt and pepper, to taste
- Lettuce leaf
- Avocado and black olives for garnishing

Instructions:

1. Cut the fish into ½ inch pieces.
2. Squeeze lime juice over the fish. Stir. Then, store in the fridge overnight.

3. Before lunch, take the fish out and drain. Add the rest of the ingredients except for the avocado, lettuce and olives.

4. Toss well.

5. Arrange the lettuce on a serving dish.

6. Lay it flat and pour the fish mixture over it.

7. Add the black olives and avocado slices for garnishing. Serve and enjoy

Nutrition Per Serving Calories: 70 Fat: 1g Net Carbohydrates: 5g net Protein: 10g

17. TACO SALAD KETO STYLE

Makes 2 salads - Prep time: 5 minutes Cook time: 12 minutes

Ingredients:

- The Salad prep:
- ¼ cup of red cabbage, shredded
- Half of an avocado, cut into slices
- 1 cup of spring lettuce
- 1 cucumber, sliced
- 2 carrots, shredded

The Taco Mix prep:

- Half of freshly squeezed lime
- 1 pound of fatty ground beef, organic and grass-fed
- 1 teaspoon of dried oregano
- 1 tablespoon of cayenne powder
- 2 tablespoons of unsalted butter, grass-fed or ghee
- Sea salt

The Avocado Dressing prep:

- ¼ cup of apple cider vinegar
- ¼ cup of MCT oil
- 1 cup of fresh cilantro, chopped
- ¼ cup of fresh lemon juice
- 2 avocados
- 4 cups of cucumber, sliced
- Sea salt
- 4 spring onions

Instructions:

1. Using a medium-sized pan, cook beef thoroughly and sauté until cooked.
2. Remove the excess fat from the pan and add cayenne powder, ghee or butter, oregano, salt, and lime juice.
3. Take pan away from the fire and just set it aside.

4. Combine the ingredients from the salad and put them onto plates.
5. Top them off with the beef mixture.
6. Place the ingredients of the dressing into a blender and mix until creamy and smooth.
7. Drizzle the mixture on top of the salad.
8. Eat and enjoy!

Nutrition Per Serving Size: 1 salad Calories: 570 Fat: 45g Net Carbohydrates: 3g net Protein: 39g

Chapter 5 Recipes. Keto Lunches

18. No Sugar Fish and Butternut Squash

Serves 4 - Prep time: 15 minutes - Cook time: 15 minutes

Ingredients:

- Squash preparations:
- A medium-sized butternut squash (seeded and peeled, chopped into 1" cubes)
- 4 tablespoons of unsalted butter, grass-fed
- 4 medium-sized peeled carrots (chopped into 1" pieces)
- Half tablespoon of vinegar, apple cider
- A spring onion (chopped into 4 slices)
- Sea salt
- 2-3 tablespoons of MCT oil

Fish Prep:

- A pound of tilapia filets
- 1/4 cup of ground coffee beans
- A tablespoon of dried oregano
- 1/4 teaspoon of vanilla powder

- 3 tablespoons of xylitol
- 2 tablespoons of sea salt
- A tablespoon of ground turmeric

Instructions:

1. Heat the oven to 320 degrees F.
2. Mix the vanilla powder, coffee beans, turmeric, xylitol, salt, and oregano in a bowl.
3. Pour over fish generously and rub the mixture in.
4. Put the fish in a dish used for baking (single-layer). Place the dish on the middle oven rack. Bake for about 8-10 minutes or until cooked through.
5. Steam the carrots and squash until tender.
6. Combine carrots and squash in a blender along with the remaining ingredients, blend to reach the desired consistency.
7. Place the puree on a plate and place fish on top. Add a side salad or other steamed vegetable for a complete a delicious meal. Enjoy!

Nutrition Per Serving Size: 1 cup Calories: 250 Fat: 45g Net Carbohydrates: 12 g net Protein: 40 g

19. SCALLOPS WITH DECADENT BUTTER

Serves 5 - Prep time: 12 minutes - Cook time: 15 minutes

Scallops are great because almost any higher end restaurant will have them on the menu, and most markets as well as club stores carry them in the fresh or frozen section. One thing to keep in mind is to don't cook them too long or they will get tough and rubbery. Scallops pack a vitamin punch as well, they have protein as well as B12 and selenium.

Ingredients:

- 1 ½ lb. Scallops
- 2 tsp black pepper
- 7 tbsp. butter
- 2 tsp minced garlic
- 2 tbsp. lemon juice
- 2 tsp Basil leaves chopped, or dried basil herb
- 1 tsp chopped thyme

Instructions:

1. Place the thawed out or fresh scallops on a dry paper towel on your counter, lightly pat them dry.
2. Heat up a large pan over medium heat and add your favorite oil.

3. Place the scallops in the pan evenly, don't crowd them together. Cook them until they are a light brown color, about 1 ½ minutes a side.

4. Once cooked, place the scallops on a plate.

5. Add the butter to a skillet and saute the minced garlic slightly for about 2-3 minutes, careful not to burn it.

6. Add the lemon juice, thyme and basil to the pan and add the scallops, toss them in this mix.

7. Serve with your favorite add in, cauliflower mash, a bed of greens with vinaigrette and so on.

Nutrition Per Serving: Calories: 320 Fat: 30 Net Carbohydrates: 3g net Protein: 20g

20. Sautéed Shrimp

Serves 2 - Prep time: 10 minutes - Cook time: 10 minutes

This is a real treat, I like to top this recipe over BBQ vegetables, or salad, or you can make cauliflower mash.

This recipe will make two servings.

Ingredients:

- 1/2 pound shrimp, peeled and deveined
- 1 tablespoon freshly squeezed lemon juice

- 1 tablespoon chopped parsley
- 1 teaspoon of olive oil
- 1/2 teaspoon herb seasoning
- Salt and pepper

Instructions:

1. Place skillet over a medium heat and add oil.
2. Stir in shrimp and sauté for 1 minute.
3. Sprinkle with salt, herb seasoning and pepper.
4. Drizzle with lemon juice and keep stirring.
5. Cook for 4 more minutes.
6. Sprinkle chopped parsley before transferring to a serving dish.

Nutrition Per Serving: Calories: 142 Fat: 6 Net Carbohydrates: 1g net Protein: 25g

21. CURRY FISH WITH COCONUT

Serves 4 - Prep time: 10 minutes - Cook time: 15 minutes

Ingredients:

- 2 tbsp. butter (add to baking to dish)
- 2 lbs. white fish, salmon is okay
- 1 tsp salt and pepper

- 3 tablespoons butter
- 4 tablespoons red or green curry paste
- 14 oz. coconut milk or cream
- 6 tbsp. cilantro, chopped
- 1 lb. cauliflower

Instructions:

1. Preheat your oven to 400°F (200°C).
2. Add the butter to grease the baking dish.
3. Place the fish in a baking dish, don't use too large a dish, you don't want the fish to have too much room.
4. Add salt and pepper to your liking, then place a tbsp of butter on each fish.
5. Mix up the coconut, curry and cilantro in a little bowl and add this mixture to the fish.
6. Bake in the oven for 15-20 minutes, not too long, fish gets dry if you cook too long.
7. Boil or steam the cauliflower and serve with fish, drizzle more sauce to your taste.

Nutrition Per Serving: Calories: 142 Fat: 6 Net Carbohydrates: 1g net Protein: 25g

22. CHICKEN AND MUSHROOMS

Serves 1 - Prep time: 5 minutes - Cook time: 15 minutes

Chicken and mushrooms doesn't get any better. This recipe is just great, I like to add a little hot sauce at the end and have a Diet Coke, yum. This recipe can make one serving or more.

Ingredients:

- 1 boneless chicken breast
- 1 cup sliced mushrooms
- 1/4 cup chopped green bell pepper
- 1 1/2 tablespoon soy sauce
- 1/4 tablespoon minced onion
- 1/2 teaspoon honey
- 1/2 teaspoon Garlic powder

Instructions:

1. Preheat the oven to 350 degrees Fahrenheit.
2. Place the boneless chicken breast in a baking dish. Top with onion flakes.
3. Mix the soy sauce with the garlic powder in a bowl and pour over the chicken. Cover the baking dish. Place in the pre-heated oven. Let the chicken cook for 30 minutes.

4. Once cooked, uncover the baking dish and add mushrooms and bell pepper on top. Cover the dish again and place it back inside the oven.

5. Bake until the mushrooms are tender. Take it out and set aside to cool. Serve.

Nutrition Per Serving: Calories: 335 Fat: 28 Net Carbohydrates: 2g net Protein: 25g

23. CHICKEN MEATBALLS

Serves 4 - Prep time: 10 minutes - Cook time: 20 minutes

This recipe is wonderful if you miss meatballs, you can add this to some low carb bread, or vegetable pasta, and you are on a roll. You can make this dish with Turkey, Ground Beef, Chicken, it's up to you.

This recipe makes 4 hefty meatballs, double up for more.

Ingredients:

- 1/2 pound ground turkey
- 1 egg
- 1 garlic clove, finely minced
- 1/8 cup breadcrumbs (made from almond flour)
- 1/8 cup of chopped onion

- 1/8 cup chopped parsley
- 1/4 teaspoon oregano
- Salt and pepper

Instructions:

1. Mix all the ingredients in a large bowl.
2. Divide into three equal portions. Shape each portion into round balls then flatten.
3. Place a nonstick pan over medium heat and spray with cooking spray.
4. Cook each side of the meatballs for about 6 minutes or until brown and cooked through.
5. Serve immediately.

Nutrition Per Serving: Calories: 270 Fat: 10 Net Carbohydrates: 3g net Protein: 30g

24. SIZZLING CHICKEN BREAST, MUSHROOM AND BELL PEPPER STIR-FRY

Serves 4 - Prep time: 10 minutes - Cook time: 12 minutes

Ingredients:

- 3 large chicken breasts, grilled and sliced into strips
- 2 small red onions, finely chopped

- 9 tablespoons olive oil ½ cup cooked spinach
- ½ cup of fresh shitake mushrooms
- 1 large green bell pepper cut into long strips
- 1 teaspoon finely minced garlic
- 1 teaspoon finely minced ginger ½ teaspoon grated lemon peel ½ teaspoon cumin
- Salt and pepper to taste
- Squeeze of lemon

Instructions:

1. In a sizzling wok, fry onions, bell peppers, and mushrooms in olive oil.
2. Add chicken strips, cumin, garlic, ginger, lemon peel, salt, and pepper to the pan and cook at high heat.
3. Remove from heat and serve beside spinach, adding a squeeze of lemon.

Nutrition Per Serving: Calories: 400 Fat: 20 Net Carbohydrates: 25g net Protein: 20g

25. Broccoli Cheesy Chicken Bake

Serves 6 (1 cup servings) - Prep time: 10 minutes - Cook time: 30 minutes

If any of you enjoy Costco food court chicken bakes, then you will love this recipe, only it is healthier. I still do enjoy a chicken bake every now and then, but this recipe is my go to for a hearty meal that satisfies. I suggest to get yourself a casserole dish for this one.

Ingredients:

- 1 head of broccoli
- Quarter of a stick of butter for frying
- 1 chicken breast
- 1 green bell pepper
- 1 yellow onion
- 2 cloves of garlic.
- 6 strips bacon
- 8 ounces shredded cheddar cheese
- 8 ounces shredded mozzarella
- 8 ounces cream cheese
- 4 ounces full fat cream

Instructions:

1. Fry the bacon on the stovetop. Put the butter into another pan and fry the chicken over the stovetop. Dice the pepper, onion and garlic. Chop the broccoli into nice bite-size florets.
2. Preheat the oven to 350 degrees Fahrenheit.

3. Add the pepper, onion and garlic to the chicken once it is nearly cooked through, in the same pan and fry them. Cut the chicken into strips and continue to fry.
4. Lightly steam the broccoli. Place in the casserole dish. Add the chicken, peppers, onions and garlic and stir to combine. Add the cream cheese, the cream and half of the mozzarella and cheddar. Stir all of these together.
5. Top the casserole with the other half of the mozzarella and cheddar.
6. Bake for 30 minutes.
7. Enjoy with a small green salad on the side.

Nutrition Per Serving: Calories: 500 Fat: 20 Net Carbohydrates: 3g net Protein: 40g

Chapter 6: Recipes. Keto Dinner

26. Stuffed Pork Chops

Serves 4 - Prep time: 10 minutes - Cook time: 60 minutes

Ingredients:

- 4 Pork Chops (get the cut you like thin or thick)
- 4 Slices Bacon
- 4 Oz. Bleu Cheese
- 4 Oz. Feta Cheese
- 4 tbsp. Green Onion chopped
- 3 Oz. Cream Cheese
- 4 tsp of Salt, pepper
- 3 tsp garlic powder

Instructions:

1. Heat a small pan, use medium heat, cook the bacon, and don't drain off fat
2. Take a small bowl and mix the Feta and Bleu cheeses together
3. Add into the bowl the bacon and green onions
4. Add the cream cheese, mix well all the ingredients

5. Slice the pork chops on the side without the fat, slice right down the side
6. Stuff the pork chops with the cheese mix
7. Use regular toothpicks to close the openings on pork chops
8. Add the salt, pepper and garlic to both sides of the chops
9. Take the same pan used earlier to cook bacon, and sear the pork chops for 1 minute a side
10. Take the pork chops and bake at 375 degrees for 25 minutes
11. Carefully remove the pork chops and serve

Nutrition Per Serving: Calories: 800 Fat: 40 Net Carbohydrates: 1g net Protein: 100g

27. PARMESAN CRUSTED PORK CHOPS

Serves 4 - Prep time: 5 minutes - Cook time: 10 minutes

Ingredients:

- 1 ½ pounds of boneless pork chops
- 1 tsp salt and pepper or to taste
- 3 tbsp. olive oil

The Crust

- 1/3 cup grated Parmesan cheese
- 1/3 cup pork rinds, crushed
- 1 tsp minced parsley,
- 1tbsp. minced garlic
- 1 tsp lemon juice
- 3 large eggs, beaten (to dip pork chops in with pork rind crust)
- 3 tsp water

Instructions:

1. Place the thawed out pork chops on your cutting board and season with salt and pepper on both sides.
2. Use a large bowl and beat the eggs.
3. Spread the cheese and crushed pork rinds onto a large enough flat surface, add the parsley and garlic and lemon juice and mix it up with hands.
4. Heat up an iron pan, pour the olive oil in and use medium heat.
5. Use your hands to dip and coat the pork chops into the pork rind crust mix.
6. Place the chops into the pan.
7. Fry the pork chops, 1 minute each side and be careful not to burn them.
8. Fry for an additional 2 minutes each side and then place them on a rack or a foil covered plate.

9. You can serve these pork chops over cauliflower mash, a bed of greens, or cut into pieces and have with a salad.

Nutrition Per Serving: Calories: 800 Fat: 40 Net Carbohydrates: 1g net Protein: 100g

28. SLOW COOKER LAMB

Serves 6 - Prep time: 5 minutes - Cook time: 5 hours

Ingredients:

- 3 lb. Leg of Lamb
- 1/3 Cup Olive Oil
- 3 Tbsp. Whole Grain Mustard
- 2 Tbsp. Maple Syrup
- 5 Sprigs Thyme
- 8 Leaves of Mint
- 2 tsp. Rosemary
- 2 tsp. Minced Garlic
- 2 tsp Salt and Pepper

Instructions:

1. Cut 4 even slits across top of lamb with a good knife.
2. Place the lamb into the slow cooker and rub the lamb down with butter or olive oil, mustard, maple syrup and then the salt and pepper.

3. Put the garlic and rosemary together packed tight in each slit you made across the top of the lamb.
4. Cook for 5 hours on medium, add thyme and mint, and then cook for additional 30 minutes.

Nutrition Per Serving: Calories: 400 Fat: 34 Net Carbohydrates: 0.2g net Protein: 30g

29. SUCCULENT RACK OF LAMB

Serves 4 - Prep time: 5 minutes - Cook time: 32 minutes

Ingredients:

- 40 oz. Lamb Ribs
- 2 tsp Salt
- 1 tsp Black Pepper
- 2 tbsps. butter
- 2 tbsps. Parsley
- tbsp. Mint (optional)
- 1 tsp Rosemary
- tbsp. minced Garlic (or 2 garlic cloves)
- tbsps. Dijon Mustard

Instructions:

1 Heat oven to 425°F.

2   Sprinkle the lamb with salt and pepper.

3   Melt the butter in a skillet or iron pan, cook the lamb on both sides over high heat for 30 seconds each side.

4   Use a bowl and mix the mint, chopped up parsley, rosemary and the garlic.

5   Brush the lamb with the mustard and pat it with the herbs mix evenly.

6   Use a roasting pan and place the lamb into it.

7   Roast the lamb for 25 minutes for medium, use less time if you like it rarer. Use a thermometer and the internal temperature of the lamb should be 120 f.

8   Let the lamb rest for additional 8 minutes before attempting to slice it in-between the bones.

9   Garnish with the rosemary and serve.

Nutrition Per Serving: Calories: 700 Fat: 60 Net Carbohydrates: 0.1g net Protein: 40g

30. BEEF WITH BROCCOLI AND CHEESE

Serves 6 - Prep time: 5 minutes - Cook time: 25 minutes

How much more simpler can you get, this one is great for a quick dinner. I like to add Velveeta cheese to the broccoli, or lots of butter and salt. It is a little twist on a Chinese style dish, but you can make it your own.

Ingredients:

- 1/4 pound round steak, cut into thick strips
- 1/4 onion, sliced into wedges
- 1 cup broccoli florets
- 1/8 cup water
- 1 tablespoon cornstarch
- 1 tablespoon of soy sauce
- 1 tablespoon vegetable oil
- 1 tablespoon water, divided
- 1/4 teaspoon ground ginger
- 1/8 teaspoon garlic powder

Instructions:

1. Mix garlic powder, cornstarch and water in a bowl. Add the steak strips. Mix well.
2. Place a skillet over medium heat and pour half the oil portion.
3. Add coated beef strips and stir fry until tender.
4. Transfer the beef strips onto a plate.
5. Then, pour other half portion of oil into the skillet and cook the onion and broccoli.
6. Cook for 4 minutes.
7. Add the beef strips back into the skillet and add brown sugar, ginger, cornstarch, soy sauce and water.

8. Stir fry for another 2 minutes. Serve immediately.

Nutrition Per Serving: Calories: 400 Fat: 15 Net Carbohydrates: 6g net Protein: 35g

31. BRAISED SHORT RIBS

Serves 4 - Prep time: 10 minutes - Cook time: 1 hour, 30 minutes

These are no ordinary short ribs, I added garlic to them which makes them have a really decadent taste. Full of vitamins and minerals beef is pound for pound a health food and with garlic you get the detoxing effects of this great food, enjoy!

Ingredients:

- 5 (5 oz. each) beef short ribs
- 2 tsp salt
- 2 tsp black pepper
- 3 tbsps. olive oil
- 2 tsps. minced garlic
- 5 tbsps. dry red wine (optional)
- 2 ½ cups Beef bouillon

Instructions:

1. Preheat your oven to 375 Fahrenheit.

2. Rub the beef ribs with the salt and pepper, add more to taste.

3. Use a oven safe skillet or deep dish pan and add the olive oil evenly to grease the pan.

4. Cook the ribs over high heat and sear in a pan for 3 minutes, then place the ribs on a plate.

5. Add the garlic to your pan or skillet and saute the garlic for 2 minutes.

6. Add the dry red wine and simmer the ribs for 3 minutes on low heat (optional, you don't have to add red wine).

7. Add the beef bouillon, short ribs, and the cooked juices from the plate back into your pan and simmer for 1-2 minutes.

8. Next cover the skillet and place in your oven and braise them for 1 hour, 30 minutes.

9. Serve the short ribs with their own juices over each serving and add your choice of sides, cauliflower mash, veggies, or some potato if you had a tough workout.

Nutrition Per Serving: Calories: 500 Fat: 40 Net Carbohydrates: 4g Protein: 40g

32. CHEESEBURGER BACON CASSEROLE

Serves 6 - Prep time: 10 minutes - Cook time: 1 hour

Casseroles are a great way to eat on the ketogenic diet, because they are super easy and fantastic if you have a busy lifestyle. The flavors of this recipe will make you think of cheeseburger heaven, they can keep in the fridge for up to a week.

Ingredients:

- 3 tbsp. butter
- 2 tbsps. minced garlic
- 1 onion, sliced
- 1.5 lbs. ground beef
- 1/2 cup pickles
- 1 tbsp. mustard
- 3 tbsp. sugar-free ketchup
- 1/2 can chopped tomatoes
- 1 ½ cups cheddar cheese, grated
- 1 tbsp. chopped parsley
- 4 large eggs
- ½ cup heavy whipping cream
- 1 tsp salt, to taste
- 1 tsp black pepper, to taste

- 7 bacon slices

Instructions:

1. Preheat your oven to 375 Fahrenheit
2. Grease a pot with the butter
3. Slice the onion and add the minced garlic to the pot and cook for 6 minutes over medium heat, keep stirring the mix so it doesn't burn
4. Place the ground beef in the pot with the onions and garlic and cook for 4 minutes until slightly browned, less if you like a little pink.
5. Add the pickles to the mix.
6. Add the mustard, ketchup, tomatoes and parsley, mix well, then take everything off the heat.
7. Use a bowl and add the eggs and cream, season with salt and pepper and use a good for or whisk.
8. Place the cheeseburger mix into a large baking safe dish.
9. Add the cheddar cheese evenly over everything, pour the egg and cream mix and stir with a wooden spoon or spatula.
10. Place everything in the oven and bake for 10 minutes at 350 Fahrenheit
11. Then top the dish with the bacon and bake for 10 more minutes at 375 Fahrenheit.

12. When finished, place over a rack and let it cool down for 8 minutes.

13. Serve with keto bread or lettuce and top with mayonnaise or sour cream and spices. Store in the fridge for up to a week, you can freeze this dish, but I recommend you don't as cream and ground beef can harbor bacteria after sitting out and cooling and restoring, be careful.

Nutrition Per Serving: Calories: 500 Fat: 60 Net Carbohydrates: 5g Protein: 40g

33. KETO BOMB CHEESEBURGER

Serves 4 - Prep time: 15 minutes - Cook time: 10 minutes

You want a cheeseburger? Me too, yumm. Now you don't need any bread for this recipe, if you like you can use the keto bread recipe or buy some wonderful eto bread. Many specialty shops and online will sell this item cheap, or make it a treat by adding your favorite fixings.

Ingredients:

- 1½ lbs. ground beef
- 7 oz. shredded cheese
- 2 teaspoons garlic powder

- 2 teaspoons onion powder
- 2 teaspoons paprika powder
- 2 tablespoons fresh oregano, finely chopped
- 2 oz. butter, for frying
- Salsa (store bought or make your own)
- 2 medium tomatoes
- 1 small scallion
- 1 avocado
- 1 tbsp. extra virgin light olive oil
- 1 tsp salt
- 1 fresh cilantro

Toppings

- 4 tbsps. mayonnaise
- 4 slices bacon
- 3 tablespoons Dijon mustard
- 4 servings of sliced dill pickles
- 4 lettuce leaves
- 4 tbsps. jalapeños sliced

Instructions:

1. Use a small bowl and chop up to your liking the salsa ingredients and toss, then set aside.

2. Mix the seasoning and only half the cheese into the beef.

3. Make 4 burger patties and fry them up in a pan over medium heat, you can alternatively grill them over a BBQ if you like.

4. Add the cheese at the end, careful to not burn the burgers, if you like a little pink cook the burgers for less time.

5. Place the burgers over the lettuce leaves individually and top with pickles, mustard, sugar free ketchup or sour cream and more jalapenos.

Nutrition Per Serving: Calories: 500 Fat: 40 Net Carbohydrates: 3g Protein: 37g

Chapter 7: Recipes. Keto Veggies & Side Dishes

34. Cauliflower Mash

Serves 1 - Prep time: 5 minutes - Cook time: 5 minutes

These are great for any side dish or all by itself. Creamy and buttery these faux mashed potatoes will knock your socks off. Enjoy!

Ingredients:

- ½ cup cauliflower
- 3 tbsps. grated parmesan cheese (or any cheese you like)
- 2 tbsp. butter
- 2 tsp lemon juice
- 1 tsp olive oil (optional)

Instructions:

1. Cut the cauliflower finely into florets.
2. Bring a pot to boil for a few minutes and add salt

3. Boil the cauliflower for 4 minutes so they are lightly firm, drain off water when done.

4. Place the cauliflower in a blender, blend medium speed for 30 seconds.

5. Add the salt and pepper, add more butter or olive oil to taste.

Nutrition Per Serving: Calories: 300 Fat: 4 Net Carbohydrates: 3g Protein: 6g

35. COLESLAW

Serves 4 - Prep time: 5 minutes - Cook time: 5 minutes

Coleslaw everyone's favorite. This recipe doesn't have carrots; if you are not as strict on your carb level you can add some carrots to this recipe.

Ingredients

- 3 cups cabbage , shredded
- 1/2 cup mayonnaise
- 3 tbsps. rice or cider vinegar
- 1 packet of Splenda, Sweet and Low or your favorite sweetener
- 1/2 tsp celery seed

Instructions

1. Start by mixing in a large bowl the cider vinegar with the Splenda.
2. Add in the mayo and celery seed and mix till you get a dressing.
3. Pour the dressing over the shredded cabbage. Toss lightly and enjoy!

Nutrition Per Serving: Calories: 60 Fat: 2 Net Carbohydrates: 2.5g Protein: 2g

36. STUFFED MUSHROOMS

Serves 4 - Prep time: 10 minutes - Cook time: 15 minutes

These stuffed mushrooms are decadent and rich. You can serve them as appetizers or add them as a side dish to your favorite meat or fish recipes.

Ingredients:

- 16 mushrooms
- 6 slices of bacon
- 3 tbsps. butter
- 8 oz. cream cheese
- 2 tbsps. chives, finely chopped

- 2 tsp paprika powder
- 2 tsps. salt and pepper

Instructions:

1. Preheat your oven to 375 Fahrenheit.
2. Use a pan over medium heat and fry the bacon until slight crisp, be careful not to burn it, once done, allow cooling, and chop the bacon up. Don't throw away the bacon fat, we will use it.
3. Clean the mushrooms by rinsing in a strainer with salt water, and remove the stems, chop them to your liking.
4. Sauté the mushrooms in a pan with the bacon fat, add some butter if you want for more fat.
5. Next place the mushrooms in a lightly greased up baking dish.
6. Place the bacon in large bowl with the mushrooms and other ingredients.
7. Add the bacon mix to the baking dish with the mushrooms and bake for 15 minutes. Keep checking so you don't burn the mushrooms.

Nutrition Per Serving: Calories: 300 Fat: 25 Net Carbohydrates: 4g Protein: 20g

37. KALE SALAD

Serves 4 - Prep time: 5 minutes - Cook time: 10 minutes

When you Sauté kale it takes on a mouthful of flavors that are sure to delight. I have added bleu cheese and garlic to make this an exciting side dish or standalone as a snack.

Ingredients:

- 3 tbsps. butter
- 1 cup kale
- 2 tsps. salt and pepper
- 1 cup heavy whipping cream
- 4 tbsps. mayonnaise
- 1 tsp Dijon mustard
- 3 tsps. Extra Virgin Light Cooking olive oil
- 1 tbsp. minced garlic
- 3tbsps Bleu cheese or feta

Instructions:

1. Use large bowl and mix the heavy cream, mayonnaise, mustard, garlic and olive oil, add the salt and pepper.
2. Rinse the kale in a sturdy strainer, remove the stems and cut into small pieces.

3. Heat up over medium a large iron pan and melt the butter, sauté the kale lightly, careful to not overcook the kale.

4. Use a large salad style bowl and pour the dressing of your choice over the top, toss lightly and serve with crumbled bleu cheese or feta.

Nutrition Per Serving: Calories: 150 Fat: 15 Net Carbohydrates: 6g Protein: 20g

38. ZUCCHINI ROLLERS

Serves 4 - Prep time: 10 minutes - Cook time: 60 minutes

Zucchini is great and a staple in my kitchen it is versatile and has endless recipe ideas add some mushrooms and you are on your way to keto wonderland.

Ingredients:

- 2 lbs. zucchini
- 2 tsps. salt
- 2 tbsps. butter
- 8 mushrooms, finely chopped
- 7 oz. cream cheese
- 7 oz. shredded jack cheese or cheddar
- 1 green or red bell pepper, finely chopped

- 2 eggs
- 1 tsp onion powder
- 1 tbsp. fresh parsley, chopped
- 1 tsp salt
- 1 tsp pepper
- ½ cup mayonnaise
- 4 oz. leafy greens (spring mix)

Instructions:

1. Preheat your oven to 375 Fahrenheit.
2. Then slice the zucchini lengthwise and place on a small line of baking sheet with a liner of parchment paper beneath it.
3. Add the Salt and let the zucchini sit for 5 minutes.
4. Place the zucchini in a baking dish and bake for 15 minutes or until soft, remove and place on a rack when done.
5. Heat up a pan over medium heat with butter, and chop the mushrooms, sauté until light brown in color.
6. Use a large bowl and add the other ingredients, half the cheese, mushrooms and toss well.
7. Cover the zucchini with the cheese atop each slice.
8. Take each zucchini slice and roll them upside down in a baking dish, add more cheese on top.

9. Bake once more for 10 minutes until the cheese gets a brownish melted color like pizza.

10. Add the mayonnaise and serve over the greens.

Nutrition Per Serving: Calories: 350 Fat: 20g Net Carbohydrates: 8g Protein: 25g

39. CREAMY SPINACH

Serves 4 - Prep time: 10 minutes - Cook time: 25 minutes

Who doesn't like creamed spinach? Well, I am sure you are going to love this recipe as much as I do. I like to make this dish for parties and even though some don't do keto they can still enjoy it with French bread as well, all welcome.

Ingredients:

- 2 tbsps. butter
- 1/3 sweet onion, thinly sliced
- 3 cups spinach, stemmed and washed, you can use frozen spinach in a pinch
- ½ cup heavy cream
- ¼ cup Chicken Bouillon
- 1 tsp sea salt
- 1 tsp pepper
- ½ tsp ground nutmeg (optional)

Instructions:

1. Heat up a large pan over medium heat and add the butter.
2. Add the onions and sauté them for about 3 minutes.
3. Add the spinach, cream, Bouillon, salt, pepper.
4. Sauté the spinach till it begins to welt, 3 minutes is plenty.
5. Serve immediately.

Nutrition Per Serving: Calories: 200 Fat: 23g Net Carbohydrates: 2g Protein: 7g

40. SESAME TOFU AND EGGPLANT DELIGHT

Serves 4 - Prep time: 10 minutes - Cook time: 10 minutes

This is a great vegan recipe that has scrumptious tofu, sesame and is sure to bring an Asian fusion taste to keto that will keep you coming back for more.

Ingredients:

- 1 package of firm tofu
- ½ cup cilantro (optional)
- 4 tbsps. rice vinegar
- 4 tbsps. sesame oil

- 3 tbsps. minced garlic
- 1 tsp crushed red pepper flakes
- 1 large eggplant
- 1 tbsp. Extra Virgin Light Cooking olive oil
- 1 tsp of salt and pepper
- 3 tbsp. sesame seeds (toasted)
- 5 tbsps. soy sauce

Instructions:

1. Preheat your oven to 250 Fahrenheit.
2. Remove the tofu from the package and rinse it off in a strainer to get the package juices off.
3. Place the tofu on a plate and press the excess water out of the tofu with a paper towel.
4. Place the cilantro, rice vinegar, sesame oil, garlic and pepper flakes in a bowl and mix well.
5. Wash the eggplant in salt water, and peel and julienne it, you can alternatively use a mandolin if you have on in your kitchen to make faux noodles.
6. Heat a up a pan over low heat and add the olive oil, cook the eggplant until it gets semi soft, or cook how you like it. Add more sesame oil to soak up the eggplant slightly.

7. Use a baking dish and add all the ingredients including the eggplant, cover with foil or a lid and place in the oven for 5 minutes.
8. Take the tofu our and cut into 7 slices and spread sesame seeds all over the plate, coat the tofu on both sides well with the sesame seeds.
9. Add 2 tablespoons of the sesame oil to the pan, then fry the tofu on both sides for 2-3 minutes each side, if you like it less crispy cook a little less.
10. Pour the soy sauce into the pan and fully coat the tofu, brown them slightly for a minute or two.
11. Remove the eggplant noodles from the oven and add the tofu on top.
12. Serve immediately.

Nutrition Per Serving: Calories: 300 Fat: 25g Net Carbohydrates: 5g Protein: 12g

41. PESTO FAUX NOODLES

Serves 5 - Prep time: 10 minutes - Cook time: 7 minutes

I love pesto anything. Nuff said! Enjoy this recipe.

Ingredients:

- 5 small zucchinis, trim off the ends

- ½ cup Pesto (any brand okay)
- ½ cup Parmesan cheese, shredded (any cheese okay)

Instructions:

1. Use a good peeler or whatever you like to use to make faux noodles.
2. Place the faux noodles into a large bowl.
3. Add the pesto and Parmesan cheese and toss well.
4. Serve and enjoy!

Nutrition Per Serving: Calories: 100 Fat: 10g Net Carbohydrates: 1g Protein: 5g

Chapter 8: Recipes. Desserts & Snacks

42. Pumpkin Fat Bombs

Makes 20 Pumpkin Fat Bombs - Prep time: 8 minutes – Refrigerate for 70 minutes

Who said because you are on a diet you can't have dessert! Not with the Keto Diet, this way of eating is real creative and is supposed to be tasty. All these recipes are sugar-free, gluten free and as always are keto friendly. I love pumpkin and I am sure you will love these dessert pumpkin fat bombs, enjoy!

Ingredients:

- 1/3 cup real butter
- 1/3 cup cream cheese
- ½ cup pumpkin puree
- 4 tbsps. chopped almonds (optional if you don't like nuts)
- 3 packets of Splenda or you can use Stevia or any sweetener you like.

- 1 tsp ground cinnamon
- 1 tsp ground nutmeg

Instructions:

1. Place parchment paper evenly in a 8 x 8 inch pan.
2. Use a large bowl and add the butter and cream cheese and mix it well till you get a smooth texture.
3. Next add the pumpkin puree and mix well.
4. Add the almonds, Splenda, cinnamon and nutmeg.
5. Pour the mix from the bowl into a large pan, use a good sturdy spatula or hard wooden spoon and spread the pumpkin mix evenly within the pan.
6. Place the pumpkin in the freezer for 70 minutes.
7. Make 20 little fat bombs and store them in a container of your choice and freeze.

Nutrition Per little fat bomb Serving: Calories: 100 Fat: 10g Net Carbohydrates: 0g Protein: 5g

43. Chocolate Pudding

Serves 7 - Prep time: 10 minutes - Cook time: 7 minutes

Chocolate pudding is a great sugar craving killer, I love it and have this all the time with whipped cream in the evening after dinner, enjoy!

Ingredients:

- 6 ounces of cream cheese
- 5 ounces of whipping cream
- 2-4 drops of liquid stevia, to taste
- 1-2 tbsp. cocoa powder, to taste

Instructions:

1. Mix all ingredients until a pudding consistency has been achieved.
2. Grab a bowl and enjoy!

Nutrition Per Serving: Calories: 125 Fat: 5g Net Carbohydrates: 1g Protein: 5g

44. CHIA PUDDING

Serves 4 - Prep time: 5 minutes - Cook time: 5 minutes

Chia Seeds are a great way to alleviate constipation; they pack a lot of vitamins. I know some of you may have the Chia Pet commercials stuck in your head, but give it a chance you'll enjoy it.

Ingredients:

- 3 heaping Tablespoons chia seeds

- 1 cup unsweetened almond milk
- A few drops stevia
- A spoonful of almond butter

Instructions:

1. Put the chia seeds into a bowl.
2. Add the almond milk and stir.
3. When a pudding consistency has been achieved add the stevia drops and stir well.
4. Top with a bit of almond butter.

Nutrition Per Serving: Calories: 200 Fat: 11g Net Carbohydrates: 1g Protein: 6g

45. COCONUT PUDDING

Serves 4 - Prep time: 5 minutes - Cook time: 5 minutes

I added Chia seed to this recipe; you can omit them if you don't like Chia. But give it a try I am sure you will like it.

Ingredients:

- 4 tablespoons chia seed
- 5 tablespoons unsweet coconut
- 1/3 cup heavy whipping cream
- 1/3 cup water

- 1 teaspoon vanilla

Instructions:

1. Put the chia seeds, coconut, water and vanilla in a blender.
2. Process the ingredients until smooth.
3. Pour the mixture into a bowl.
4. Let it chill in the fridge for 15 to 30 minutes or until thick.
5. For additional flavor, you can also sprinkle the pudding with nuts.
6. Enjoy!

Nutrition Per Serving: Calories: 200 Fat: 11g Net Carbohydrates: 1g Protein: 6g

46. BLUEBERRY MUFFINS

Serves 6 - Prep time: 10 minutes - Cook time: 20 minutes

Now you must be saying, OMG, muffins, no way? Yes way, I just love this recipe. Enjoy them in the morning with coffee, or anytime.

Ingredients:

- 2 cups of almond meal

- 1 teaspoon baking soda
- A few drops of lemon extract
- 1 cup of full fat cream
- 2 eggs
- ½ stick of melted butter
- A few drops of stevia
- A handful of blueberries

Instructions:

1. Preheat your oven to 350 degrees.
2. Combine the almond flour and the baking soda.
3. Add the cream and mix with a hand mixer.
4. Add the eggs one at a time and mix. (If the mixture seems too thick, go ahead and add another egg).
5. Add the drops of stevia and lemon extract and mix.
6. Fold in the blueberries carefully into the batter.
7. Fill muffin cups halfway full in a muffin pan and bake for 25 minutes, or until the muffins are golden brown

Nutrition Per Serving: Calories: 220 Fat: 20g Net Carbohydrates: 2g Protein: 10g

47. LEMON BALLS

Serves 6 - Prep time: 10 minutes - Cook time: 20 minutes

Ingredients:

- Zest of 1 big lemon
- 1 cup of desiccated coconut
- 1 cup of cashews, raw
- Sea salt
- 1/2 tsp. of natural vanilla extract, concentrated
- Extra desiccated coconut for garnish
- 2 tbsp. of maple syrup

Instructions:

1. Mix all the ingredients in a blender or a food processor.
2. You can add more desiccated coconut if desired.
3. Shape the mixture into balls and store in the fridge to freeze.
4. Serve cold.

Nutrition Per One Lemon Ball: Calories: 55 Fat: 6g Net Carbohydrates: 1g Protein: 10g

48. FUDGE BALLS

Makes 35 Balls - Prep time: 8 minutes - Chill time: 1 ½ hours

These Fudge Balls are what can I say? Excellent! The ketogenic diet as you have seen has a lot of treats and this recipe is a sure treat. You can stay comfortably in ketosis while eating them and still burn the fat, and best of all they are grain free, gluten free, dairy free, vegan, and best of all have no sugar, wonderful.

Ingredients:

- 1 ½ cup almond butter
- ½ cup coconut oil
- 1/2 cup cocoa powder, sugar free
- 1/2 cup coconut flour
- ¼ tsp Splenda, Stevia or your favorite sweetener

Instructions:

1. Heat up a pot over low to medium heat, melt the coconut oil first then add the almond butter.
2. Keep stirring and then add the coconut powder, coconut flour and sweetener and stir well.
3. Use a large bowl and pour the mix in and place it in the freezer for 1 hour.
4. Check back on the mix it should be formed now and set, remove the mix from the bowl and form balls (have a little bowl of cool water next to you and wet

hands a little when forming the balls as coconut oil can get messy from heat).

5. Use a flat tray or any favorite baking pan and return the balls to the freezer, let them sit for at least 40 minutes.

6. Enjoy!

Nutrition Per Fudge Ball: Calories: 150 Fat: 14g Net Carbohydrates: 1g Protein: 3g

49. SNICKERDOODLE COOKIES

Makes 15 cookies - Prep time: 10 minutes - Cook time: 8 minutes

Ingredients:

- 1 ½ cups almond flour
- 1/3 cup coconut oil
- ¼ cup maple syrup, sugar free
- 1 tbsp. vanilla extract
- ¼ tsp baking soda
- Splenda packets to taste or 6 Stevia Drops (use your favorite sweetener)
- Dash of salt
- 1/3 cup Macadamia Nuts

Instructions:

1. Preheat your oven to 350 Fahrenheit.

2. Use a large bowl and combine the coconut oil, maple syrup, vanilla and sweetener.

3. In a small separate bowl, combine the almond flour (use different flour if you don't like almonds), baking and salt.

4. Now add 1/3 Cup of Macadamia Nuts to a food processor of your choice.

5. Grind the macadamia nuts into a course like state.

6. Mix in the Macadamia nuts and coconut oil, maple syrup, vanilla and sweetener together until you get a doughy texture.

7. Take a small bowl and mix 2 tbsps. of Cinnamon and 1 tsp Erythritol and set aside.

8. Roll the dough mix into balls of your liking depending if you want big cookies or small.

9. Roll the balls gently around in the cinnamon mix until there lightly coated, then lay them onto your counter and use the bottom of a nice size glass jar and flatten the balls our into a semi thick cookie.

10. Grease a baking tray with some butter and bake them for 8 minutes, they won't look done at first, this is okay, once they are out of the often and begin to cool they will look like Snickerdoodles :)

11. Allow them to cool and eat with your favorite sugar free latte or drink enjoy!

Nutrition for 1 Cookie: Calories: 140 Fat: 13g Net Carbohydrates: 2g Protein: 4g

50. KETO STRAWBERRY ICE POPS

Makes 8 ice pops / Prep time: 10 minutes, 3 hours freeze time /

Ingredients:

- 1 ½ cups strawberry, frozen is fine or fresh
- 1 cup of coconut milk or use mascarpone (optional)
- 1 cup whipping cream
- ¼ cup Splenda, Stevia or your favorite sweetener.
- 1 tsp vanilla extract

Instructions:

1. If using fresh strawberries, wash them in a strainer with cool salt water and cut off the green parts, if frozen skip this part.
2. Put the strawberries in your favorite blender and add the coconut milk and vanilla extract.

3. Use pulse mode for 10-20 seconds until smooth, don't do too much, and remember less is more.

4. Break out your favorite Popsicle molds and add your sticks.

5. Place the pops in the freezer for 2 -3 hours, more if necessary.

6. Check on the pops after a few hours and remove them from the freezer, put them in your favorite storage container, they will keep for a month or so.

Nutrition for 1 Popsicle Calories: 170; Fat: 12g; Protein: 5g; Net Carbs: 2g

51. NO FUSS BLUEBERRY CHEESECAKE

Serves 12 / Prep time: 10 minutes / Cook time: 25 to 30 minutes

No bake blueberry cheesecake is perfect for beginners. There is no need for a base and these can be made as one large cheesecake or poured into little individual teacups.

Ingredients: Mix for the Base

- ¼ cup butter melted
- 2 tsp Splenda powder or your favorite sweetener
- 1/8 cup coconut desiccated and shredded

- 3/8 cup almond flour or your favorite

Cheesecake Filling

- 1 ½ tbsps. gelatin powder, Jell-O is fine
- 2 cups boiling water
- 2 tbsp. Splenda, powder
- 2 tsp berry extract
- 2 cups cream cheese, brick type that doesn't spread, full fat.
- 1 cup blueberries fresh or frozen is okay

Instructions:

1. In a small bowl mix the butter and sweetener together.
2. Then add the almond and coconut and mix that.
3. Press this mix into a greased up flan dessert dish and place in the fridge while you ready for making the topping.
4. Place the Jell-O in the 2 cups of hot water and stir gently
5. Next add the cream cheese, flavoring and sweetener, and use a hand blender to really whisk it smooth.
6. Use the same hand blender and puree the berries, make them smooth as well.

7. Add everything together in the same large bowl and stir well.

8. Pour everything onto the base and then place in the fridge.

9. You can add whip cream on top, more berries or your favorite topping, have some good coffee and you are good to go.

Nutrition Per Serving Calories: 250; Fat: 23g; Protein: 10g; Net Carbs: 3g

Chapter 9: Recipes. Keto Sauces & Condiments

52. Avocado Butter

Makes 2 cups / Prep time: 20 minutes, plus 2 hours chill time

Avocado is a fantastic keto food; it has a healthy dose of good fats such monounsaturated fats, oleic acid, and omega-3s.

Ingredients:

- 1/3 cup butter
- 1-2 avocados, peeled, pitted, and cut into chunks
- Juice of 1 lemon
- 1 teaspoon chopped cilantro
- 1 teaspoon chopped fresh basil
- 1 teaspoon minced garlic
- 1 teaspoon salt
- Dash black pepper

Instructions:

1. Put the butter, lemon juice, cilantro, basil, garlic and avocado into a processor of your choice and mix until smooth.
2. Add the salt and pepper to taste.
3. Transfer the butter onto some parchment paper and shape it gently into a small roll tightly.
4. Place the butter roll still in the paper into the fridge and let it set for about 2 hours, more if needed.
5. Top your favorite keto bread, meats or eat straight away.
6. This butter will keep fresh in the fridge for 2 weeks.

Nutrition Per Serving (1tbsp) Calories: 20; Fat: 10g; Protein: 8g; Carbs: 1g; Fiber: 1g; Net Carbs: 0g

53. BERRY BUTTER

Makes 2 cups / Prep time: 15 minutes

This is really a great recipe and if you enjoy farmers markets like I do, then you'll love it. Remember you can use strawberry, boysenberry, and berry really you enjoy for this recipe.

Ingredients:

- 1 ½ cups shredded coconut

- ½ tbsp. coconut oil
- ½ cup fresh berries
- ½ tbsp. freshly squeezed lemon juice
- 1 tsp pure vanilla extract
- Instructions:
- Put the coconut in a blender and mix until its smooth, 3 mins is good.
- Next add the coconut oil, berries, lemon juice, and vanilla extract to the coconut butter and mix until very smooth,
- Store the berry butter in your favorite container in the fridge for 3 weeks.
- Serve butter over your favorite keto bread, meats, and salads or eat it straight away.

Nutrition Per Serving 1tbsp Calories: 22; Fat: 3g; Protein: 7g; Carbs: 1g; Fiber: 2g; Net Carbs: 1g

54. BALSAMIC DRESSING

Makes 1 cup / Prep time: 3 minutes

Usually I like to buy dressings as it is much easier to have on hand, many brands now are organic and sugar free. We all may have a busy lifestyle so adjust accordingly, this recipe you will enjoy, Balsamic is such a tasty dressing for salads and it sits well, don't worry about a little sugar in the vinegar it isn't a big deal, as long as you are strict mostly with your meals, don't give it another thought.

Ingredients:

- 1 cup light tasting extra-virgin olive oil (the dark green bottled ones are too heavy in taste for this recipe)
- 1/3 cup balsamic vinegar
- 2 tbsp. chopped
- 1 tsp oregano
- 1 tsp chopped basil
- 1 tsp minced garlic
- 1 dash of salt
- 1 dash of pepper

Instructions:

1. Use a medium sized bowl and mix the olive oil and vinegar, about 2 minutes.
2. Next mix the basil, oregano and garlic
3. Add the salt and pepper to taste.
4. Place the dressing into your favorite container and store in the fridge for 2 weeks, make sure to give it a shake before use.

Nutrition Per Serving 1tbsp Calories: 15; Fat: 2g; Protein: 8g; Carbs: 1g; Fiber: 2g; Net Carbs: 1g

55. KETO RANCH DRESSING

Makes 2 cups / Prep time: 6 minutes

Ranch dressing, what else is there to say. Its creamy taste good over a house salad or with hot wings and we love it. This is a staple in my kitchen, now you can buy many great brands that are sugar free and some that are super low in carbs, but give this Ranch recipe a try, you're gonna love it.

Ingredients:

- 2 cups mayonnaise
- 1/3 cup sour cream
- ¼ cup heavy whipping cream
- 1 tablespoons dried parsley
- 1 teaspoon dried dill
- 1 teaspoon garlic granules
- 1 teaspoon onion powder
- 1 teaspoon basil
- 1teaspoon pepper

Instructions:

1. Put all ingredients in your favorite food processor.
2. Blend the ingredients for 60 seconds
3. Pour into your favorite container and refrigerate.
4. Ideally you should let everything sit in the fridge overnight as the ranch will take on a real nice flavor, but you can serve right away as well.

Special Tips

If you don't own a food processor or you just want speed in cooking and no fuss, then place all the ingredients in a bowl and stir and mix well.

Nutrition Per Serving Per 1 Tbsp.110 Calories, 12g Fats, 0g Net Carbs, 2g Protein.

56. VEGAN MAYONNAISE

Again there are a lot of vegan mayonnaises for sale; however it's nice to know you can make your own. Here is my best recipe I use.

Time: 5 minutes

Makes: 2 cups

Ingredients:

- 1/3 cup soymilk (preferably unsweetened)
- 1 cup canola oil
- 1 lemon, juiced
- 1 teaspoon cider vinegar
- ½ teaspoon salt (Morton's)

Instructions:

1. For this recipe you will use the blender or your favorite food processor by adding first the soymilk, then the lemon juice, cider vinegar, and salt.
2. Blend on medium speed for about 2 minutes.
3. Reduce the speed on the blender to low and slowly add the oil of your choice.
4. Once you have poured all the oil, change the speed to high and blend for one more minute.
5. Next place the mayonnaise in a favorite container and place in there refrigerator for about two weeks.
6. Again feel free to experiment with different flavors and spices until you find a mix you really love and enjoy.

Nutrition Per Serving 1tbsp Calories: 22; Fat: 10g; Protein: 8g; Carbs: 1g; Fiber: 0g; Net Carbs: 1g

57. THOUSAND ISLAND DRESSING

Makes 2 cups / Prep time: 6 minutes

Thousand Island dressing usually is packed with carbs, and many think you just can't have it anymore on the Ketogenic diet. Boy are they wrong, get ready for the best tasting thousand island you ever had.

Ingredients:

- 2 cups mayonnaise
- 3 Tbsp. Sugar free ketchup
- 1 Tbsp. apple cider vinegar
- 3 Tbsp. diced pickle
- 2 Tbsp. diced onion
- 1 tsp powdered Splenda or Stevia to taste
- 1 tsp salt
- 1 tsp pepper

Instructions:

1. Chop the pickles.
2. Dice finely the onion.
3. Place all ingredients (but leave out 1 tbsp. each of pickles and onions diced), in a food processor.
4. Blend for 45 seconds.
5. If you don't have a food processor, then place everything in a bowl and mix well.

6. Add back the 1 tbsp. of diced onion and pickles in the dressing and stir well.

7. Pour the mix into your favorite container and place in the fridge for about 2 hours.

Nutrition Per Serving Per 1 Tbsp.100 Calories, 15g Fats, 0.5g Net Carbs, 1g Protein.

58. CAESAR DRESSING

Makes 2 cups / Prep time: 8 minutes, plus 15 minutes cooling time / Cook time: 5 minutes

Caesar dressing is just a fantastic dressing. However, many on the market today have a lot of nasty ingredients lurking in them, from MSG to glute and hidden carbs. Get your Caesar dressing on now with this easy to make recipe.

Ingredients:

- 3 teaspoons minced garlic
- 5 large egg yolks
- 1/3 cup wine vinegar
- 1 tbsp. dry mustard
- 2 splashes of Worcestershire sauce
- 1 cup extra-light cooking virgin olive oil
- ¼ cup lemon juice

- Salt and pepper to taste

Instructions:

1. Heat up a small pan over medium heat, and then add the garlic, vinegar, egg yolks, mustard and Worchester sauce.
2. Stir while cooking the sauce, once it thickens up and bubbles, remove the sauce from the pan. Allow it to cool for about 8 minutes.
3. Place the pan mix to a bowl and whisk adding in the olive oil.
4. Add the lemon juice, and add the salt and pepper to taste.
5. Put the dressing into your favorite container and place in the fridge.
6. The dressing will stay fresh for up to two weeks.

Nutrition Per Serving (2 tablespoons) Calories: 200; Fat: 30; Protein: 6g; Carbs: 2g; Fiber: 0g; Net Carbs: 1g; Fat 98%/Protein 1%/Carbs 1%

59. HOLLANDAISE KETO STYLE

Makes 2 servings / Prep time: 5 minutes, 5 minutes to cool

I love Hollandaise sauce, and if you're thinking this sauce will be difficult to make, it's really easy. We will use a microwave for this one, it's fast, super simple and ready in minutes. You can also add tarragon chopped to the sauce if you like it béarnaise style. As always have fun and make the sauce your own.

Ingredients:

- 1/2 cups butter salted
- 3 egg yolks
- 3 tsps. Water (cold)
- 1 small lemon, juiced or 4 tsps. Lemon juice store bought, use it to taste.
- Dash of salt
- Dash of black pepper or cayenne.

Instructions:

1. Take a large bowl and beat the egg yolks, lemon juice, salt and pepper (optional), slowly add the butter while continuing to mix.
2. Microwave the sauce for 10 to 30 seconds, remove and whisk it slightly during the heating.
3. If the sauce starts to separate, add a few tbsps. of water and whisk slightly.

Nutrition Per Serving: 300 calories; 25 g fat; 0.5 g carbohydrates; 3 g protein

60. KETO PESTO

Makes 1½ cups / Prep time: 10 minutes

I love pesto, and if you make keto noodles or enjoy this sauce as much as I do you'll know what I mean. Feel free to add to this recipe if you wish, you can add Kale, spinach or your favorite greens to the mix or make it tangy, have it your way. You can also impress your friends and family even if they don't follow the keto diet, they will love it too.

Ingredients:

- 1 cup fresh basil
- 4 garlic cloves
- 2 teaspoons yeast
- 1/3 cup light tasting extra-virgin olive oil

Instructions:

1. Place the, basil, garlic, and yeast in your favorite food processor and set it to pulse, mix until everything is finely chopped for about 2 to 3 minutes.
2. Let the processor keep running and add the olive oil and pesto, the mix will start to get thick and pasty like.
3. You can add 3-4 tbsps. or water if the sauce gets to thick.

4. Store the pesto sauce in your favorite container for up to 2 weeks.

Nutrition Per Serving 2 tbsps. Calories: 50; Fat: 3g; Protein: 3g; Carbs: 1g

61. BEEF & CHICKEN STOCK

Makes 10 cups / Prep time: 15 minutes /

Cook time: 11 hours, plus 25 minutes cooling time

I usually buy my beef stock as there are many great companies that use organic ingredients and do not have preservatives or other nasties. But it is nice to make your own beef stock from time to time. Try this recipe out, you will love it and so will your friends and family. This recipe will call for beef bones, that may sound kind of funky at first, where will you find beef bones? Actually many supermarkets have beef bones ready available, look near the butcher section or meat section of your market, you can also go to a local butcher and ask them for beef bones they will be more than happy to accommodate you.

Beef Stock Ingredients:

- 3 lbs. beef bones (any bones will do, knuckles, ribs, etc.)
- 7 black peppercorns
- 3 thyme sprigs
- 4 garlic cloves, peeled and crushed
- 3 bay leaves
- 2 carrots, washed and chopped into 1 ½ -inch pieces
- 2 celery stalks, chopped into small chunks
- 1 onion, peeled and chopped
- 1 gallon water
- 1 tsp. light tasting extra-virgin olive oil

Chicken Stock Ingredients:

The beef stock and chicken is the same preparation and cooking time; the only difference is you must buy two whole chickens, and you can discard the bones after cooking the stock if you wish.

Instructions:

1. Preheat your oven to 375°F.
2. Place the beef bones in a pan and roast for 25 minutes.
3. Transfer the bones to a crockpot or stockpot.
4. Next add the peppercorns, garlic, thyme, bay leaves, carrot, celery, and onion.

5. Add the gallon of water; be sure that the water covers the bones.

6. Use high heat setting and then let it boil, reduce the heat after 10 minutes and let the stock simmer or a bit, about 3 minutes.

7. Next you should check the stock for 2 hours it is cooking, remove the foam that forms at the top by skimming it.

8. Let the stock simmer for Simmer for 11 hours, then when finished remove the pot from heat, cool for 25 minutes.

9. Remove bones you don't want in the stock with some sturdy tongs, and strain the stock with a mesh sieve. You can throw away the vegetables and bones if you want.

10. Place the stock in your favorite containers and store in the fridge for up to a week, the stock will last in the freezer for up to 3 months.

Nutrition Per Serving 1 cup. Calories: 70; Fat: 6g; Protein: 8g; Carbs: 0g

SPECIAL TIPS ON EATING OUT

This is what you have been waiting for, just how do you eat when you are at a restaurant or on the road. What about food labels? And appeasing sugar cravings? For the most part the Keto Diet is pretty easy to do and you can eat anywhere almost anytime. Now I say "almost" anytime because if you are trying to lose that weight and your just starting out I don't recommend that you make it a weekly thing by going to your favorite pasta restaurant and load up on the bread and noodles thinking you can go back on the diet and lose it anyway. Once you lose all your weight and find your carbohydrate comfort level you can get away with this often and not gain the weight back, but for the mean time you should be careful.

The ease and practicality of the diet makes it enjoyable and I can't honestly say that about most other diets that leave you out in the cold when it comes to dining out, and that can be a pain when it comes to friends and family. This became important to me when I designed the Keto Diet, when losing weight it can be hard enough, and making things easier is the number one priority.

Remember when you followed the low fat high carb diet and you had to know the menu beforehand and you had to find out if it "fit in" with where you were with numbers and so on.

If a certain dish was low fat, how many calories, let's just say you weren't the waiter's friend that day. Maybe you even opted out and didn't go altogether and missed out on an opportunity to spend time with your loved ones or even meeting someone new for a relationship. You never have to experience this with Keto, you can relax now.

And best of all Keto is very convenient, no matter what Fat Loss Plan you follow or what day of the week it is or where you are in the world, you always will find meat and vegetables. Let's say you go out to eat with friends and you just started The Ketogenic Diet, okay, you really want to lose weight but you don't want to seem like a weirdo and impose any new diet plans you have, so you go, okay there is pasta in the menu and it's your favorite, well can't have that one, now you always liked steak but you shied away because of the saturated fat and lies you been told by the "experts" so you get the 20 oz. Ribeye with garden vegetables and butter melted on top, and you skip the mashed potatoes and order a diet coke. Now with that meal no one will criticize you. And you will be doing your health a justice. Even your favorite fast food restaurants are not off limits either, go to your local burger joint and order the burger, huge with no bun or fries and add your favorite diet drink and your losing weight. It's just great! Compare this to a low fat high carb diet at any restaurant and you will have a hard time ordering anything delicious, I guarantee it.

For most of us the temptation can be too great and if you fall no problem, remember that The Keto Diet is forgiving and you will still lose weight. Life is all about balance and well some things are out of our control, I know I said no alcohol, but if the occasion calls for it and you are with that special someone go for it. Remember everything you do has to be fun. Life will throw a curve ball at us out of nowhere and things will come up such as; holidays, your best friends' wedding , your children's parties and birthday cake, business meetings, a long getaway and vacation with that special someone. Disneyland, and just about anything you can think of. No matter what you still want to lose weight, I know that and you know that, but you have the best plan right here in your hands and you win every time, I will be with you every step of the way.

Why it's Important to Know How to Eat in a Restaurant

Remember that it only is most important to be careful eating out when you are trying to lose weight not maintaining. Once you reach your target weight and you find your carbohydrate comfort level then when you go to a restaurant and you want shrimp pasta with garlic bread it shouldn't be a problem you simply go right back to your usual comfort carb level and you won't gain weight. In the beginning though you have to exercise caution because your metabolism is not yet accustomed to burning body fat for energy and you will halt weight loss. This is not desirable so be patient.

What If you're Still Tempted?

I know you are in the middle of your fat loss plan and your trying so hard and you feel tempted to have that cheesecake and coffee, what do you do? Well you're not alone and this doesn't mean your weak. We are human, eating out and with others is a natural part of our lives, its social and normal, and that you get to rejoin the human race while still keeping true to your goals of losing weight and getting healthier. The best firepower you have is your mind. Everything is going great you lost 50 pounds and have 20 more to go and then you decide to eat out with friends and all of a sudden they want to order dessert and your favorite is right in front of you, that chocolaty, gooey, fudge explosion, with a bug ole scoop of vanilla ice cream and that hot coffee to go with it. So what do you do? Do you bite the bullet or the spoon, and say no, or do you derail all your weight loss and cave in and say "Oh it's just this once." Well being prepared is the best thing you can do, prevention is the best medicine they say. Remember that none of this really applies unless you are in a fat loss plan, or close to your target weight. Otherwise anything goes while sticking to your comfort carbohydrate level for maintenance.

Here is what you can do

Sticking to your guns and not going off the diet, knowing you just have few more pounds to go, and then you can have it any time.

Decide to eat whatever you want and have that pizza and breadsticks, with soda, or try that dessert you love.

Appease sugar cravings with diet sodas, or order a low carb dessert (most restaurants have low carb dessert options).

Remember whatever you decide you always win with the Keto Diet because no other diet plan can promise weight loss and as quick. So even if you decide that your going to have that high carb meal, no problem just go right back to eating high fat and reducing your carbs appropriately to the carb level according to the carb level you picked. This actually can boost your mood especially if you have been strict with your carbs for at least a few weeks, and the beauty is that when once you have switched your metabolism to becoming a fat burner and not relying on carbohydrates (sugar) for energy anymore you won't get fat, it's almost impossible.

Out and About Eating

The Ketogenic Diet you will find is much easier than most other diets where you are stranded in diet limbo for who knows how long. No matter what restaurant of fast food place you love they will always offer steak and shrimp with garlic butter, or salmon and greens. Sit back and relax you have reached dining bliss. You pretty much have nothing to think about just browse the menu and you're off.

Depending on what carb level you set for yourself, anything pretty much goes, unless you are trying to lose weight and not in maintenance. Sometimes situations are out of your control, so let me guide you on what to do in social situations.

At a family dinner party, your parents may have fixed you your favorite meal and you know how parents are you never grow up in their eyes, so do you just go all out and eat that lobster pasta she made you, or do you in front of many explain you new eating plan and make yourself the center of attention, well I like balance in everything I do, look at it this way you love lobster pasta with garlic bread and your mother went out of her way to make it, so yes please eat the food and then some, your not going to magically gain the weight you lost, your body is in fat burning mode, and once you are at home all you have to do is go right back to reducing your carbohydrates and any mishaps or weight gain will never happen, and you make your family happy and yourself in the process.

When it comes to being at work, you can simply pack a lunch with your favorite low carb goodies, but it really depends on how high you want to take your carbs that day, say you set your carb level at 40 grams a day, but your eating Chinese food with friends, one bowl of jasmine rice tops out at 45 grams net carbs, what should you do? Skip the get together and make up an excuse, or just go and make a bad show not eating because you're frustrated and worried about the carbs and blah blah. No, please don't do this, have fun, maybe allow yourself one bowl of rice and eat it slow, and go to town on the veggies and meat, or maybe you will make just dinner at this restaurant a happy time and eat everything, this perfectly fine, just go back on keto when your home. You will learn what that carbohydrate sweet spot is for you, where you can still maintain your weight and eat carbs a little higher and you have more wiggle room with the carbs. Say, when its lunch time at work and everyone wants to order a pizza, well are you trying to lose more weight or are you maintaining, or perhaps you just have 10 pounds to go till you reach target weight, if you are maintaining then go right ahead and eat as many slices as you want and then go right back to reducing your carbs after that last meal, simple right. No stress and no worries just simply either reduce your carbs later or take down the count.

You will find that there is more freedom with the Keto Diet when it comes to eating out, if your out eating with friends just eat whatever you want, enjoy yourself, your not going to gain 50 pounds by eating at Sizzlers this weekend. Weight loss should be easy, and smooth no pains. If you're trying to lose weight and you eat out all the time just be patient and stick to low carb options and take into account the carb count in your journal. No need to tell the waiter anything or become the outcast because of your new way of eating. Go all out when it comes to eating out, nothing but weight loss is coming your own way don't be brainwashed.

Trust me, when it comes to eating out and following a reduced carbohydrate diet nothing could be easier and you will even find new great places to eat. I know hundreds of places in San Francisco and the bay area that serve the best lobster, N.Y. Strip steak, crab and the like accompanied with fresh vegetables cooked your way. When it comes to weight loss and permanently keeping it off you've come to the right place.

What About When Traveling?

By boat, train, car, or air it makes no difference you can enjoy many of your favorite foods and not have to preplan anything. Say you book a flight to China and you forgot to check the menu and all the food is carb based, okay no problem just go with the flow, eat whatever the food is and go low carb when you get to china I am sure you wont have a hard time finding reduced carbohydrate meals when in China. I have traveled to Asia many times and have never found it difficult to eat a reduced carbohydrate diet. Remember you are not going to magically gain weight after a days' worth of eating carbs. No matter how you are traveling enjoy yourself, life is meant to have fun and have it your way

COOKING MEASUREMENT CONVERSION CHARTS

Liquid Volume

US STANDARD (OUNCES) and METRIC (APPROXIMATE)

2 tablespoons = 1 fl. oz. = 30 ml

¼ cup = 2 fl. oz. = 60 ml

½ cup = 4 fl. oz.= 120 ml

1 cup 8 fl. oz. = 240 ml

1 ½ cups = 12 fl. oz. = 355 ml

2 cups or 1 pint = 16 fl. oz. = 475 ml

4 cups or 1 quart = 32 fl. oz. = 1 Liter

1 gallon = 128 fl. oz. = 4 Liters

Dry Volume

US STANDARD and METRIC (APPROXIMATE)

¼ teaspoon = 1 ml

½ teaspoon = 2 ml

1 teaspoon = 5 ml

1 tablespoon = 15 ml

¼ cup = 59 mL

⅓ cup = 79 mL

½ cup = 118 mL

1 cup = 235 mL

Temperatures for Oven Cooking

FAHRENHEIT (F) CELSIUS (C) (APPROXIMATE)

250°F = 120°C

300°F = 150°C

325°F = 165°C

350°F = 180°C

375°F = 190°C

400°F = 200°C

425°F = 220°C

450°F = 230°C

Scale Weight for Food

US STANDARD and METRIC (APPROXIMATE)

½ ounce = 15 g

1 ounce = 30 g

2 ounces = 60 g

4 ounces = 115 g

8 ounces = 225 g

12 ounces = 340 g

16 ounces or 1 pound = 455 g

RESOURCES

Websites and Cool Low Carb Sites

https://www.dietdoctor.com/ Dr. Andreas Eenfeldt M.D. is a Swedish doctor who specializes in Ketogenic Dieting, he won't try to sell you anything and his site is non profit even though it has .com on the end. Check him out he's great.

https://thenoakesfoundation.org/ Tim Noakes is a scientist and great man who is pioneering in the low carb community. He is at the forefront of controversy with many professional organizations because he tries to better the health of many people with diseases and the sugar industry hates that. Check out his site for the latest research into keto and the low carb world.

https://www.adaptyourlife.com/ Dr. Eric Westman M.D. heads the Duke University "No Sugar No Starch" way of eating, he has long been involved in the research of Keto, he knows his stuff and was even a personal associate of Dr. Robert Atkins M.D.

http://garytaubes.com/ Gary Taubes, author of Why We Get Fat, doesn't need a bio, you probably have heard of him, his site is great because he gets to the heart of the lies and myths surrounding Low carb, keto and how the sugar industry as well as doctors and "experts" are contributing to the many diseases we have today.

Books

Taubes, Gary. Why We Get Fat: And What To Do About It. (2010) Anchor Publishing.

Atkins, Robert M.D. Dr. Atkins' Diet Revolution: The High Calorie Way to Stay Thin Forever (1972) D. McKay Co; 1st edition

Taubes, Gary The Case Against Sugar (2016) Anchor; 1 edition

Pasquale D. Mauro M.D. Radical Diet (2007) Dr Mauro Di Pasquale; 3rd edition

Westman Eric M.D. and Moore, Jimmy. Keto Clarity: Your Definitive Guide to the Benefits of a Low-Carb, High-Fat Diet. (2014) NV: Victory Belt Publishing.

These books are fantastic, there is a lot of misinformation when it comes to Keto and low carb, these books will help you to understand how everything works when it comes to the science and history stuff, and best of all they touch on many of the problems you may run into down the road when doing low carb or keto.

Apps

MyFitnessPal (app for android and Iphone) I really like MyFitness pal, it's super easy to use and has a bar code checker for food labels, and you can track carbs or calories with ease.

CONCLUSION

From here on out, you will maximize your potential, build the body of your dreams, live with vitality, where are you going next?

The Future and You

For many of you that have lost the weight that you have been striving for so long to lose, it seems like a miracle, and it is. They say a journey of a thousand miles begins with a single step, so won't you join me in total dietary bliss. I want to leave you with some recommendations that I think you will find useful:

1. Remember that fresh vegetables and all kinds of meat, along with fruits are the most energy packed foods you can eat. You don't need anything else. Try to stay away from refined carbohydrates and packaged foods with a long list of ingredients. Unless in a mass phase. You control what goes in your mouth and simple is always best.

2. Be careful once you reach your target weight to not eat to excess even though you can lose weight just as quickly table sugar, honey, jams, cakes, pies, chips, bread, and sodas, flour

and anything else that puts on the pounds. Make sure to read those labels.

3. Make the diet your own. Try new things, go to ethnic restaurants, even if they have carbs, don't worry about it. Variety is the spice of life. This will keep you motivated and positive to keeping the weight off.

4. Have fun with loved ones, you only live once. Eat as you wish. Happiness plays a big part in weight loss and longevity. Stress is major contributor to illness so eliminate as much as you can. Maintain a positive attitude at all times.

7. Remember to stay away from drugs and alcohol, they don't help you in the long run and rob you of life. A Keto Diet can help you gain control and quit addictions.

8. Don't overdo exercise, and always have fun.

The Keto Diet is made to help you lose weight, gain control of eating habits, be more positive and have tone, and muscle and a body that you can be proud of. You never have to worry about gaining back the pounds ever again. This is not a yo-yo diet or a fad, but a way of life that will give you back what has been robbed of your LIFE. From here on out, I want to say good health to you and your family and all your dreams will come true. Live with vigor.

Would You Do Me A Favor?

You're Fantastic For Reading My Book; I Ask One Small Favor. . .

And finally, if you liked the book, I would like to ask you to do me a favor and leave a review on Amazon. I check all my reviews and love to hear feedback. It brings me great joy to hear how everyone has benefited from this book.

http://bit.ly/ketode

Thank you and good luck!

38826630R00078